For my own good luck charms -
Robert, Evelyn, Byron, Autumn and Wolfy

TABLE OF CONTENTS

Introduction
What is a charm?
One definition is that a charm is any instrument, object or set of words endowed with power via the user's will and superstitious belief. In other words, a charm is tool facilitated by the power of superstition.

So, what then is a superstition?
Contemporary thinkers with unquestioning confidence in science might well sum up superstitions as being nothing more than a set of ideas and pattern of behaviors devised by the ignorant or fearful to explain and hopefully control the world around them. These rational thinkers assert that believers in superstitions are simply not enlightened.

On the other hand, there are people who throughout human history who have seen superstitions in a completely different light. For them, superstitions evolve directly from the human knack for observation and willingness to understand the workings of the world around us. It is these individuals that humbly embrace a fundamental law which asserts everything in the physical plane is connected, and that every action has its inevitable effect on something else. Thus, in their opinion, the human race developed and followed certain actions and activities in order to live in practical harmony with what observational evidence has concluded. For these individuals, this is natural science at work.

Wherever you stand on the view of superstitions and the charms birthed from them, superstition often teaches us as much or more about the culture they emerge from than any dry history lesson could ever offer. In this respect our modern, highly technologically-reliant world is no different than the culture of ancient Egypt or the societies of medieval Europe. Anyone that assumes the modern world has dispensed with superstition as readily as it has the erection of stone pyramids and the building of castle moats really hasn't been paying attention!

The superstitions and charms presented in this book are believed in and practiced in our contemporary world. Some of these are handed down from our grandparents' time and for varying reasons remain popular, but most have evolved independently of generational tradition. These modern beliefs and practices reflect the concerns, needs, desires and views of today's generation. Learning about them can be educational for the curious, the true believer, the respectful skeptic, and even the most cynical disbeliever.

It is my aim that in addition to learning about contemporary superstitions by reading this treasury, you will be entertained. Please bear in mind that none of the material found here is intended to replace or substitute the advice of your doctor or medical practitioner, nor is anything found within these pages intended to make you discard using common sense in your everyday activities. I hope you will enjoy what you find here, and whatever motivation prompted you to open this book will be wholly satisfied!
~Regards, Beth Perry

I. Modern Charms & Superstitions, A-thru-Z

Abalone
Shells of the Haliotidae family of mollusks are called abalone, and it is from this that mother-of-pearl is extracted. This attractive shell is believed to stimulate fertility in anyone that comes in proximity to it, and as well induce feelings of tranquility to anyone touching it.

A container or box inlaid with abalone is rumored to possess the ability of making itself invisible to burglars. Such boxes are also said able to unveil themselves to the legitimate owner looking for it.

Angry words and heated arguments are said to shatter the gentle abalone.

Abraham Lincoln
The United States' 16th president is admirably remembered for his noble achievements while Commander-in-Chief, and as well for the his life having been tragically shortened by an assassin's bullet. It is no surprise that superstitions have arisen regarding this historic figure. As Lincoln was a great orator, if you plan to make a public speech, it is suggested you carry an image of Abraham Lincoln so your words will inspire others.

Misfortune is said to befall anyone that utters the name of the 16th president in the same sentence as the surname *Mudd*.

If you pass a portrait or image of Honest Abe and see a tear rolling down his cheek, it is believed you have an enemy close by.

Any U.S. copper penny found to have patina formed over Lincoln's profile is believed to bring good fortune for the person carrying it. To give such a penny in a charitable contribution is said to bring untold blessings for the person(s) receiving your donation. To wear or otherwise carry one of these pennies while serving in the U.S. military is believed to protect the individual from injuries to the head. Because of this some service members keep the patina covered penny in one of their boots.

Accountants

Some accountants make the habit of placing a newly stamped quarter in their right shoe (face side of the coin against the sole) before commencing work on a new project. This habit is thought to protect the accountant from the dishonesty of clients.

Actors (stage, theater, film and television)

For centuries the world of theater has abounded with superstitions. While some of these are still honored, new ones continue to evolve.

To see among the theater audience an unrecognized man wearing a straw hat and carrying a blue handkerchief in a vest pocket is a sign that one among the play's actors will reach the summit of thespian ambition. If the stranger is accompanied by a woman in a polka-dot dress, more than one of the performers will realize this success.

Contemporary actors still follow tradition by insisting their peers and admirers say, "break a leg" before a performance, as the saying of "good luck" is thought to bring just the opposite.

According to some modern television actors, it is thought that to indulge in a single cookie before the filming of a scene will add a very noticeable extra ten pounds of weight on screen.

It is thought among some thespians that to speak the name *James Dean* at a party will bring on a fatal vehicular accident for one among the guests. Likewise, to speak the name *John F. Kennedy* or just *JFK* while riding in an open car is said to incur bad luck if the rider is romantically involved with a blonde actress.

One should never overhear or speak the name *Sharon Tate* without immediately uttering, "Golden angel". To neglect saying this is said to bring on the notice of dark forces.

It is said that to appear in any performance adapted from a written novel or story draws the interest of the Muses. Therefore, to speak unkindly of the author during the filming or staging of the performance is thought to usher in a five-year bout of bad luck for the speaker.

If you land the role of Ebeneezer Scrooge in any play, show or film, it is recommended you give generously to charities or beggars, lest you be punished with financial ruin.

The carrying a photo of Lon Chaney (senior) while getting your make-up on is believed to encourage an excellent performance.

For a successful career it is advised to visit Mary Astor's grave at Holy Cross Cemetery in Culver City and rap politely on the actress's grave marker.

To avoid a sequence of unsuccessful dalliances and unhappy marriages, some actors sleep with peacock feathers under their mattresses.

To ward off being showed up by a fellow actor, a steaming cup of non-sweetened tea with lemon juice should be kept nearby whenever practicing your lines.

To avoid messing up one's lines, it is suggested to suck on a sprig of rosemary before a performance. If rosemary is not available, whispering the name of the first character you remember from Shakespeare's *Romeo and Juliet* before the performance or practice is thought to provide the same safeguard.

Airline peanuts
If you enjoyed a safe flight on a plane, it is said that future journeys can go just as smoothly if you bring along an unopened pack of peanuts received from that flight.

Altoids® (tin boxes)
Altoids were originally invented in the 1780's by the London-based Smith & Company and sold as a remedy to

remove poisons from the stomach. Today Altoids are popularly used as breath mints, but they are also as well known for the tin boxes they are typically sold in. Perhaps because of the general novelty of tin containers in today's plasticized world, these tins have earned a bit of a supernatural reputation. When used to store items (once the mints are gone) such items are said to never vanish, and according to belief, money kept in these tins will always make its way back to the owner if the tin is stolen.

American witches
For a Salem witch, a bayou magic woman and an Appalachian wise woman to meet under the same roof augurs three certainties: the Salem witch will emerge humbled, the bayou magic woman will walk out wealthier, and the Appalachian wise woman will carry out the Key to heaven.

Apple
From Biblical myth to Arthurian legend and on into today's romance books, the humble apple has been honored as a symbol of both temptation and true love. Slicing an apple horizontally and sharing the slices with another is believed to make them see the best in you. If the slices given come from a red apple, this is believed to enhance the physical attraction between the two of you.

To take a bite of an unblemished apple and discover a worm means you will soon see or hear from someone you'd hoped was out of your life for good.

Dipping apple slices in milk before consuming them is supposed to increase the eater's fertility.

Eating cooked yellow apples is thought to clear the memory and keep it sound.

Smelling green apples is supposed to bring fond memories.

APPS
Many warn that downloading a mobile app with one's name brings bad luck.

If you download an app with your mother's name it is said you will always have enough to eat.
See also Internet

Appliances
The purchase of a brand new appliance is usually a satisfying event. However, consider naming all new appliances before their first use to insure they provide quality lifetime-warranty performance.

Appliance repairs
Appliance repair people sometimes take a sip of anise liqueur to avoid testy or bickering customers.

Artists (and their work)
One tradition maintains that kissing a new canvass before putting the brush to it will insure a minimum of interruptions during the work.

A sculptor is said to lose a day of their natural life every time they say "ninety-nine cents" during a sales negotiation.

Some artists believe that when choosing a model for a portrayal of Jesus Christ, the model must possess three traits: 1. be a recovering alcoholic or drug addict, 2. have divorced or unmarried parents, 3. have a relative (close or distant) who has been charged at one time or another with the crime of murder. To select a model that doesn't meet these requisites is supposed to make the artist indolent and careless of their project.

Never paint snow-capped mountains in the summertime, else someone close to you will suffer an embarrassing accident come winter.

Drinking beer while sketching a nude is said to dull one's skill.

To protect your art brushes from theft and bristle loss, give them each a name, but be sure not to reveal these names to another living soul.

For success in your art, keep a depiction of chrysanthemums created by another artist in your studio.

To encourage feelings of love from a reluctant party, add your spit to the next paint you mix, and while applying it to the canvass say, "Vincent, Vincent, turn (*name of your desired*) to me, that my love they clearly see." (This one undoubtedly was inspired by the personal life of painter Vincent Van Gogh)

If you come to the realization that you have been been stingy or mean-hearted in the treatment of others and genuinely wish to improve yourself, try copying the signature of Walt Kelly in a repetitively but leisurely manner. To write or copy his signature is said to promote generosity and all-around commonsense when dealing with other people. Note, Walt Kelly was the creator of the popular comic strip, *Pogo*.

One is cautioned to never comment that Andy Warhol was an artist without making the quotation marks gesture as you speak. Failure to do so is thought to make you gullible and easily separated from hard-earned money.

To give as a housewarming present a framed Molly Hatchet album cover by artist Frank Franzetta (actual album, poster or lithograph) is thought to fail robbers that may try entering one's residence. To wear a tee shirt with one of the album covers printed on it is supposed to safeguard any male from impregnating a bridesmaid. For a woman to sleep on a pillow case with such an album cover printed on it, she will have prophetic (and amorous dreams) of a future lover.

Attorneys
Cultural belief suggests an attorney should never bring a lawsuit against their own mother, for it will usher in personal sorrows beyond measure.

For a prosecutor to wear blue shoes while trying the accused is said to bring a satisfying verdict, but one that will be reversed on appeal.

According to American folklorists, lawyers that enter a court house with a toad in their pocket will know unexpected good fortune. These lawyers may share their good luck with any child by touching or rubbing the top of the child's head.

Defense attorneys hoping to win a case for someone they know is guilty are encouraged to rub the head of a black-haired Irish child the morning of the first day of the trial. Similarly, it is said that a district attorney who has knowingly caused the execution of an innocent person can only avoid going to hell by showering a poor Irish family with food and clothing.

In the United States, attorneys and judges selected by the President are advised against kissing babies for three days after their appointment. Otherwise, they are supposedly doomed to have exceptionally ugly descendants.

Authors
To write an original fictional story with Edgar Allen Poe as one of the characters is thought to bring an unexpected change of luck for the author. However, whether this change is for the better or worse cannot be predicted.

Some readers claim that after speaking the name of writer Anne Perry one should spit over their left shoulder to avoid inviting violent thoughts. This custom may have come about due to the scandal surrounding the writer when she was just a teen - as before becoming a successful crime mystery novelist, Anne Perry was known as Juliet Marion Hulme. In 1954 Hulme and her friend Pauline Parker were convicted of the planned murder of Parker's mother.

Some people scrupulously refrain from speaking the name Peter Benchley while at the beach or when snorkeling. Benchley was of course, the author of the shark thriller, *Jaws.*

To read anything by Ernest Hemingway while drinking alcohol is thought to bring on depression.

To invoke the name of author Virginia Woolf five times in succession is alleged to bring on thoughts of suicide.

Buying a book by author and convicted murderer, Michael Peterson is said to usher in marital discord.

It is said that to receive the blessings of the writing Muses, one should obtain a river rock or some other smooth stone, ink and an owl quill. With the quill and ink, scribble the name J.K. Rowling all over the stone and the gift of skillful story crafting will be granted.

Babies
Most everyone loves a baby! It is thus no surprise many beliefs surround our innocent young:

To kiss a baby while campaigning in a political election brings favors from the gods of your country.

If you discover a lock of your baby's hair has been braided while they sleep, this means fairies are keeping watch over them.

To chase the family dog out from under a crib will make the infant fussy. But to lure the dog out with bacon omens good tidings for the family.

According to Norse beliefs, to be cruel to any infant or child under fourteen years of age will get you a long stay in Hela's punishment dungeons. To burn or mutilate your own infant or child will bring you an even lengthier imprisonment. And to kill your own infant for the sake of convenience condemns you to wander the icy road of lost souls forever.

To provide an infant delightful dreams, it is recommended to burn baby's breath incense in their room before they go to sleep. The same may be accomplished by scattering baby breath flowers under their crib or mattress.

To ward off the development of cradle cap, carve the depiction of a furry bear at the head of the crib.

Feeding a toddler boiled and finely crushed pumpkin meat is said to promote the development of strong teeth .

To protect babies from the torment of ill-tempered ghosts, let them listen to the lullabies of Johannes Brahams. To help infants develop their intellect, play Mozart as well.

To leave a swaddled babe by itself is said to bring dire consequences for the neglectful parent. And to shout at or to scold a swaddled infant is said to bring likewise unwanted consequences for the guilty party.

To help your baby have a healthy childhood, it is advised to regularly (and gently) blow on their bellies and make funny sounds.

Finding a single flea on your infant's scalp means you will soon be visited or otherwise contacted by a bill collector.

It is rumored if someone brings your baby the gift of a *Mickey Mouse* doll or another gift with the image of *Mickey Mouse* on it, you should stomp your right foot three times or else your child will grow up to have a squeaky voice and exert a generally annoying effect on others. On the other hand, if someone gives your baby an *Eeyore* toy or an item with an *Eeyore* image, they will grow up to be kind and selfless individuals.

To insure a successful life for your child, feed them a spoonful of Neapolitan ice cream on their first birthday.
See also Irish Twins

Back To The Future (movie)
It is believed that sleeping with a model of Doc Brown's DeLorean under your pillow will bring the gift of prophecy.

To extend a youthful appearance, some recommend keeping a photo of Michael J. Fox in his role of *Marty McFly* in the wallet or purse.

Balloons

To spread joy to others, release a yellow balloon to the sky on a Tuesday afternoon. Whoever eventually finds the balloon will find cheer.

There are Christians who claim that releasing a blue balloon to the elements on Good Friday helps spread the Christ's mercy among the human race.

To pop a balloon by mistake means someone you value has forgotten you.

For a red balloon to cross your path is thought an omen that the Norse villain Loki is looking to recruit you into his maleficent army.

Bartenders

Bars, pubs and taverns are popular hang-outs, and there are several beliefs about those who work tending them:

To wear an ascot while tending a bar is said to drive customers away.

Bartenders who have a shamrock tattoo on the back of their left hand are rumored to have learned their trade at the devil's pub, and as well are said to make the best Irish whiskeys around.

A bartender that wears a blue and white striped shirt along with a bow tie is thought apt to water down the liquor.

You are advised to avoid ordering a drink from a bar keep who dons a handlebar mustache, a red tie and a solid black shirt as they are supposed to be sneaky. More importantly, never let him set eyes on your gal or else you will lose her to his seductive charms!

Baseball
One is advised never to polish a glove received from a favorite pitcher, as to do so will wear away the pitcher's luck.

Catching a "spit ball" will bring swift and unpredictable changes to one's circumstances.

If you have never played baseball in your life and make a winning gamble on a game, you are at risk of one day inheriting a shamefully made fortune or legacy. However, the shame will not be associated with your own reputation if you give half of the gambling winnings to the needy.

To burn your tongue on a peanut while your team is leading is supposed to be a good omen.

It is not advisable to purchase or otherwise possess a uniform worn by any member of a team you have cursed, as to do so is said to bring numerous incidents of bad luck.

To make love on the pitcher's mound after his team played a winning game is said to make for a night of unrivaled carnal pleasure.

Some maintain that any stadium watcher who doesn't eat a hot dog during a game is inviting rain.

Basketball
A piece of a basketball hoop or goal that was broken by a player of a winning team is believed to be lucky.

To possess a towel given to a basketball player by his mother is thought to instill calm during times of domestic havoc.

For a man to blow a basketball referee's whistle at a passing woman is thought to bring bad luck into his life.

Cashews eaten during a basketball game are thought to turn against your stomach if your team loses.

Baths & showers
To inadvertently take a bath in water where a baby has urinated is said to add ten years to your life.

Never use a stranger's shower pouf, as this is said to invite any negativity they have shed directly into your own life.

Brushing your teeth while showering is said to give you renown as a delightful conversationalist.

Bear
The bear has long been held in high regard by various cultures, and several beliefs about this iconic animal have both remained and evolved in our modern world:

Possessing a bear paw instills courage in the owner.

Bear claws hung about the neck give protection against physical violence.

Meditating on images of bears is thought to help one overcome timidness.

Mothers who wear aprons with images of bears are thought to rule the proverbial roost in their domestic life.

Making love on top of a bear skin or a blanket with bear images is supposed to insure the man will be a pleasingly dominant lover.

Anyone wearing a belt buckle with a bear image will ferociously defend their family.

Bed
An unmarried person that fails to make their bed three days in a row will soon meet a lazy lover.

A married person that lets the bed go unmade for three days in a row attracts petty arguments between them and their spouse.

In positioning your bed, some believe healthy rest is best achieved by sleeping in a bed that faces eastward. For the bed to face the west is thought to entice illnesses which can bring about premature death.

To find a mouse roaming on your bed is a sign your capacity for charity will be tested.

Throwing red rose petals on a coverlet before making love is said to petition Aphrodite's blessings upon the union.

Bicycling
To speak the name of disgraced athlete Lance Armstrong while bicycling is said to bring about a string of embarrassing situations for the rider.

If you want to put cards in your bicycle spokes, be sure never to use the Old Maid from this deck of the same name. To use this spinster is said to bring about riding accidents.

If you are riding your bike on the street or sidewalk and pass by a funeral procession, whisper "Go, crows, go!" so Death won't pursue you. (*see also Crows*)

Birthday candles
Celebrating one's birthday by blowing out candles set out on a cake is now almost a universally accepted practice. By custom, the number of candles the celebrant blows out is equal to the years of their age. Before blowing out the flames, the celebrant makes a silent wish, then blows the candle flames. If all the candles are extinguished with one blow, it is said their wish will come true.

Bluebird
If in winter a bluebird perches on a tree next to your home, you may expect many happy changes to your circumstances by spring.

To you come across an orphaned bluebird egg but are unable to return it to the nest, gather sticks and grass to make a nest for it.

Now place this nest with the bluebird egg in your kitchen windowsill. This is said to entreat Frigg, Norse goddess of hearth and home, to keep your kitchen safe from fire and negative feelings. If not the windowsill, try the hearth mantle or a cabinet nearest the central most part of the home. In one of these places the nest and egg will surely attract Frigg's patronage.

Blue-raspberry flavored candy
The unexpected gift of any kind of blue-raspberry flavored candy augurs a bright and satisfying week ahead. However, you must eat the candy for the augury to come true.

Books
The books of Laura Ingalls Wilder and Charles Dickens should never be placed on the same bookshelf together as this is believed to usher in domestic disputes. This belief may have sprung from the fact Wilder was devoted to her husband until her death at the age of 90, whereas Dickens divorced the mother of their ten children in order to marry a much younger woman.

To pass along a copy of Kahlil Gibran's *The Prophet* to anyone going through grief is said to bring unexpected blessings -of an unexpected nature- upon you; however you must give the book without the intention of receiving anything for the blessings to come.

It is thought that by opening a copy of George Orwell's *Animal Farm* to a random page and then selecting a sentence by randomly pointing to a paragraph, grants you keen social insights. To do the same with a copy of Dr. Seuss's *Oh, The Places You'll Go* will give you insight to your individual purpose in life.

For a cup or glass of milk to fall for any reason while you're reading through a Betty Crocker cookbook, you will soon be visited by unexpected and hungry guests.

To mail a soldier or otherwise gift them with a copy of J.R.R. Tolkien's *The Silmarillion* is believed to keep the soldier from fatal peril while serving their country.

Reading aloud Edgar Allen Poe's *The Gold-Bug* is thought to boost one's ability to decipher codes.

Bra (brassiere)
If the underwire of your bra suddenly breaks this is a sign someone unpleasant will soon enter your life.

To feel your bra strap snapped when nobody is about means someone is jealous and is focusing negative thoughts your way.

For your breast to itch intensely under your bra for no apparent reason signals that a friend is trying to contact.

If your bra strap inexplicably breaks while you're wearing it, this is an omen of coming problems with relatives.

If your bra rides up one breast while at work, one of your co-workers has a crush on you. If it rides up both breasts not only do you have an admirer, someone else resents you for it.

Breakfast pastries
To nibble your breakfast pastry into the shape of a buffalo and then bury it in the earth is said to bring money.

For a stranger to accidentally take a bite from your breakfast pastry means destiny has brought the two of you together.

Breastfeeding
Contemporary view suggests you will enjoy a productive day if the first person to greet you is a breastfeeding mother.

It is warned if you are a man and reproach a woman for breastfeeding in public, you will be dealt incontinence for your arrogance. If you are a woman reproaching the breastfeeding mother you will receive an ovarian cyst for your intolerant conduct.

To wean your infant with as little stress for them as possible, offer in a saucer a little of the breast milk to the first cat you come across.

If your breast milk regularly soaks through your bra and into your clothing, this is thought to mean you will become pregnant again within the next nine months.

To breastfeed while standing on a dock or peer is ill-advised as it is thought to draw hurricanes.

Some people strongly believe that the dead spirits of a woman's family are often seen in photographs taken of her while breastfeeding.

Breath
To see breath moisture form on a mirror -and you know the breath isn't your own- is a sign you are being watched by the dead.

Bubble blowing (soap bubbles)
Step outdoors on the first day of spring and blow bubbles toward the sun to invite it's blessings on your life.

Your private messages may be carried to a departed loved one by blowing bubbles at their grave.

To blow bubbles onto a child's head at their first birthday is said to make them grow up honest and even-tempered.

Blowing bubbles on your pet's back will insure the animal will find its way home if it ever gets separated from you.

Among Christians, to open a Bible while blowing bubbles skyward is thought to carry one's prayers straight to the ears of Jesus.

Bucket list

The making out bucket lists, especially of things you enjoy or that make you happy, is thought to ward off any bad vibrations sent your way.

Burrito
It is said a poor keeper of secrets is the person who finds a worm in their burrito.

Butterflies
The butterfly is renowned for its gentleness toward other living things, and so it is no surprise mankind has superstitions and beliefs about this creature:

Make a wish on the first butterfly you see in the spring, for this butterfly is believed to take the wish straight to the ears of the gods. If this first butterfly is white and alights on you, it is said you are favored by the elven folk..

According to Scandinavian lore, women who were murdered by abusive husbands and babes who died of abuse, neglect or abortion are reincarnated as butterflies by Freyja. These souls are further believed able to journey back and forth between Earth and Vanaheim (Freyja's realm) in their butterfly guise. In Vanaheim, these souls enjoy all the comfort and delights they were denied during life.

It is said the woman who wears denim pants with patches or print of butterflies on the back pocket will be remembered for her wit and femininity.

For a butterfly to alight on you while you're giving someone a butterfly kiss is believed an omen you will become famous.

Cab drivers
It is cautioned you should always take care not to mock a cab or taxi driver's accent, or else you will get a hole in the sole of a favorite shoe.

Cab drivers that help deliver a baby or stop an act of crime will know ease and luxury in their next life.

Cactus plants

If you like growing cacti and don't want to invest in expensive grow lights, the best place to keep your plant is a place where it receives the full strength of the eastern morning light. This is not only healthy for the plant, it is thought to help spread the energetic vibrations of the cacti throughout your home.

Calendars

A calendar that doesn't have the dates for the full and new moons will bring many doubts to the owner.

Some contend that domestic unhappiness is drawn to any home where birthdays of family members are not noted on the calendars.

Cards (regular playing cards)

If you are wary of the intentions of others, carry the Jack of Clubs. This is said to open your third eye and enable you to distinguish truth from lies.

Carrying a Joker card in your wallet or purse is believed to thrust your best personality traits forward.

If you are a woman and wish to conceive, sleep with the Queen of Hearts either under your mattress or in your bed clothing. This Queen is thought to attract fecund blessings.

To win the love of a certain individual, give them the Two of Hearts card and without a conversation about it. To speak of the card will neutralize the charm.

Burying the Ten of Hearts near your doorstep or placing it under a stone near the outside of your door will eliminate any curse which has barred loved from reaching you. Additionally, the Ten of Hearts is believed to generally draw and aid in the development of freely given and lasting affections.

Carrying the Ace of Spades is thought to draw chaotic fortunes of an unpredictable nature. Handle with care.

Carrying the Queen of Clubs is reputed to bring success for artistic ventures.

Carpenters
When a carpenter is about to take a spouse, they should be the one to carve the headboard of the marriage bed. Once the wedding takes place, the newlyweds should knock three times on the headboard the night of their wedding and before the union is consummated. This act is supposed to spare the couple from knowing financial hardship.

Cars and other vehicles
To stumble while exiting a car or truck is a sign you just avoided some fatal vehicular accident.

Hanging from the rear-view mirror a piece of wood naturally perforated with a hole is deemed helpful in guarding one against the temptation to drive recklessly.

Images of sexy women on truck mud-flappers are thought to keep the driver safe from murderous hitch-hikers.

One is cautioned to never buy tires that were mounted on a vehicle involved in a fatal accident, as spirits of misfortune are rumored able to hide in rubber until they decide to act again. Similarly, some people refuse to acquire any vehicle involved in a fatal accident as they are considered "death bait".

Cashier
Always treat a good store cashier with courtesy, as failure to do so will draw problems for you on the return home.

Cat collar
The wearing of a cat collar sends out the message the wearer is aloof and graceful. If a bell is hung from the collar, the wearer also evokes a kittenish sexual aura.

Cats

For the last couple of decades cats have taken and kept the global popularity award when it comes to household pets. Accordingly, several new beliefs about cats have infiltrated our culture!

A cat staring at a wall is thought to be watching beings from other dimensions.

Cats have the power of seeing the auras of all living things, so if one is staring funny at you don't be alarmed.

If your cat walks across your keyboard, this is a sign you've been spending far too much time on the computer.

Still popular is the superstition that a black cat crossing one's path brings misfortune. Those that believe this advise that the misfortune can be crossed out by immediately drawing an X in the air.

A cat that shows up at your door having escaped a "crazy cat lady" will bring accolades to your family.

Cats that do absolutely nothing cute while being filmed are said to be more intelligent than others.

Feeding a cat ice cream or frozen treats with the intention of giving them a headache will bring you injuries involving the skull.

A cat that habitually chases scraps of wadded paper is said to be the reincarnation of a writer or playwright.

It is said anyone drowning kittens is condemned to shovel the devil's litter box in hell - and be advised, his dark majesty's cat weighs half a ton and eats every thirty minutes!

:Cedar
Aromatic cedars have been used for centuries in the making of furniture, incense, keepsake boxes and other types of containers. The scent of aromatic cedar wood -of practically every variety- is still believed to bring back pleasant memories.

Constructing for your child a toy box made of aromatic cedar is also thought to invite the spirits of benign elementals to take up residence among the child's toys.

Cell phones
When someone drops their cell phone and it cracks, it is said that they have missed an opportunity. If you are the person who finds the cracked cell phone, the opportunity will find its way to you.

Champagne
It is a well-known custom to break a bottle of champagne over the bow of a boat or ship before it sets sail for the first time so that the maiden voyage is a safe and successful one. However, some believe that to substitute non-bubbly for the champagne will promote the opposite effect.

Drinking champagne in which meadowsweet has been steeped is alleged to cool the urge to commit infidelity.

Car and motorcycle racers are advised to never share celebratory champagne with a brown-eyed virgin, or she will end up breaking their heart.
(See also New Year)

Channel surfing
To see the number 13 in an ad or other presentation flash across the TV screen while channel surfing is a warning that an annoying or harassing person is searching for you.

To catch a glimpse of yourself watching and/or using the remote control while channel surfing -a glimpse that cannot be attributed to an ordinary reflection on the screen- is a warning you've just seen your doppelganger (one's ethereal double, or ghost). Sightings of doppelgangers have long been said to mean imminent death for the individuals who encounter one.

Cherry stems

One belief that has been popular over the last few decades involves cherry stems: any woman who can put a cherry stem in her mouth and tie it in a knot with just her tongue and teeth is destined to be a most talented lover!

Childbirth
To assure an easy labor for friend or loved one, open in the delivery room a can or bottle of soda pop that has the mother's name printed on it. Also, whoever drinks from this soda pop will develop a strong or unusual relationship with the baby.

Children's imitation-flavored beverages (from mix-it packs)
Uninvited house guests are said to be hard to get rid of if you offer them the cherry flavored variety of these type of beverages.

To make a grumpy relative easier to deal with, give them a glass of orange imitation-flavored beverage; just be sure you've secretly taken a sip from their glass before handing it to them.

Clay
If you seek to keep an unwanted visitor from returning to your home again, sprinkle clay dirt over the path they leave on.

To take genuine red Georgia clay out of the state is said to attract the curiosity of extraterrestrials to yourself.

Mixing together a whole broken egg (including shell), milk and clay dirt and pouring this mixture at your front and back doors is thought to draw friendly elves. This mixture -when poured under your bedroom window or put into a stone bowl under your bed- is also believed to entice spirits of fertility and procreation into your life.

Clouds
For a purple cloud to appear amid white ones denotes coming prophetic dreams for the observer.

To notice the unusual sight of your initials or name appearing in the clouds means great and marvelous changes are coming into your life.

Clover (and clover blossoms)
To find a red clover blossom stuck on the inside of your shirt, blouse or dress is a warning that a friend has urgent need of your comfort.

For a red clover blossom or leaf to be found in your hair means more relaxing days are just ahead.

For a red clover leaf to get stuck on your lip is said to mean you will have many grateful lovers.

Finding a a white clover blossom stuck to your arm is said to be a warning you carry an illness without apparent physical symptoms.

An infant or toddler found with white clover blossoms stuck to their diaper or clothing signifies they will soon have a new sibling.

Clowns
If you are thinking of choosing clowning as a career, remember that to intentionally take the stage persona of a deceased clown is known to bring sorrows. To purposely take the stage name of a deceased clown brings financial ruin.

To visit a dead clown's grave and leave a thank-you note in disappearing ink is held to be one of the highest of honors the living may bestow on a clown. Squirting the grave with a trick water-spewing flower ranks highly, too.

Keeping a clown's rubber nose under your child's bed is said to help the child develop a sense of humor.

If you see two clowns cross an intersection from opposite sides, take this as warning a thief has their eye on your shoes.

Possessing a figurine of a hobo clown is said to instill empathy toward others.

Clowns who die shortly after cheering a sick, injured or disabled child is said to be taken immediately into the arms of angels and in fact, become angels themselves. If you sight a clown with light pink hair, wearing pink shoes and gold stripes and as well carrying a single blue rose and/or a lamb, it is believed you are seeing someone's guardian angel.

Clowns -or anyone dressing as a clown- should never terrorize children. To do so condemns them to reincarnation as a manure shoveler.

Cobalt blue glassware and vessels
Serving friends beverages in glasses or vessels that are cobalt blue in color is believed to strengthen relationships.

To accidentally break a cobalt blue glass, dish or bowl is to put a friendship in jeopardy. To shield your relationships from this bad omen, immediately blink twice and trace a fingertip over your lips after you've broken such a vessel.

To serve your family on cobalt blue dishes is believed to cure any cold or flu running its course through the family.

Cockroaches
If you find a live cockroach in your clothing or see one crawling across the bed is a sign that rain with hail is headed your way.

Coffee
Keeping a coffee bean in your wallet is said to keep you from making unwise business ventures.

A person that habitually blows on cold coffee (as if to cool it) is thought to be a hypochondriac.

If you accidentally pour your coffee into a cup already containing tea, or vice versa, it is said you will soon be faced with making a tough choice.

A gnat found swimming in your coffee means members of your family are arguing about you.

People who frequently stir their iced coffee with a piece of cinnamon are thought to be trustworthy.

If you have a habit of buying an iced coffee and forget to drink it while it's still cold, family needs are first on your list of priorities.

Computers
Using a picture of running horses as the background on your monitor is said to keep the entire system running swiftly.

Some believe that images of red fish on a screen-saver brings about electrical surges and fires.

Cowlicks
People with distinct natural cowlicks in their hair are believed to possess high intelligence and sensitive natures.

Cracks
Still prevalent among juveniles is the cautionary adage, *Step on a crack, break your mother's back!*

If the glass in a photograph frame inexplicably cracks in your presence, it is said you will soon hear dire news from or about the person in the picture. If the person in the photograph has already passed on, expect to learn something shocking or unexpected about them.

One is warned to never share a pudding in which the surface has cracked; to do so will likewise cause a rupture in the relationship.

Crickets
Many cultures throughout the centuries have believed that crickets bring good   fortune, and thus discourage the killing of any crickets that enter a home. Evolved from this belief is the more recent practice of mercifully bestowing the nickname

Cricket on friends who seem to attract more than their fair share of bad luck. Likewise, infants and children who suffer from serious illnesses are sometimes nicknamed *Cricket* to provide them good luck in conquering the disease.

Crows
Crows have long been regarded in many cultures as harbingers of Death. Some believe crows have been given the office of selecting those who are about to die, while others credit them as angels assigned to carry the souls of the recently deceased to their respective afterlives.

To hear crows spatting means they are arguing over who should die next.

If you find you are being followed by a crow, it is suggested to make a X sign at the bird in order to protect your life.

For a murder (group) of crows to congregate about you, clap your hands over your head and say, "Dark angels go away! Time to meet *(your God's name)* is not today!"

Cucumbers
Cucumbers have a phallic shape, so don't be startled to learn that to burp after eating one means you have a dirty mind!

Daisies
Daisies have long been associated with innocence and affection. People still divine their beloved's affection by plucking daisy petals. Begin this act of divination by plucking the first petal while saying, "He (she) loves me", the next by saying, "He (she) loves me not". Continue in this alternative way until all the petals are removed from the daisy head. If the last petal plucked is a "He (she) loves me", then you are assured that they do.

The making of daisy chains is a tradition among girls and women, and the exchange of daisy chains is a way of bonding a friendship. To make daisy chains, pick several and loop/interlock the daisy heads through the stem of the next daisy (use your fingernail to cleave the stems) until the chain is necklace-length. Attach the last daisy to the first and the chain is complete.

Dandelions
The blowing of fluff from a single dandelion in order to fulfill a wish is a common childhood practice that stays with many of us into adulthood. Some believe that to obtain the wish, you should make it silently and then blow on the dandelion; if all the fluff loosens and scatters in one exhale then your wish will come true. Others assert you are allowed up to three attempts, but if any fluff remains on the dandelion after the third blow then your wish is destined not to come true.

Desk (work desk)
Unless it is a matter of company policy that prohibits the placement of photographs on an employee's work desk, it is said those who keep no photos on their desks lead questionable or disreputable lives.

Dogs
There are several modern superstitions surrounding man's legendary best friend:

For a dog to bark aggressively at a seemingly invisible thing in the room is thought to indicate they are trying to drive away evil spirits.

If a dog nips at its own tail three times in succession, a vehicular accident is doomed to happen on the nearest street or road.

Dressing a dog in your dead infant's clothing is said to invite the child's soul to come and stay near you.

For a strange Pekepoo to follow you home and then continue walking toward the east is a sign of coming money.

If you film the abuse of any dog without interfering or calling authorities, demons will attack and torment you in your sleep.

A strange yellow Labrador found lying at your door or front step is thought to be your guardian angel come as a visitor.

Kicking a dog out of anger incurs the wrath of Odin and Thor. Abusing or mercilessly killing a dog will keep you out of Valhalla.

One may cure a stomach ache or menstrual cramps by cuddling a Jack Russell puppy.

Waving smoke of sandalwood incense in a dog's face is said to bring prophetic visions to the smoker and to relax the dog.

It is believed that a parent who shows more affection to their dog than their child will die bitter and alone.

Giving a dog a sip of your birthday wine is thought to strengthen the bond between the two of you.

If, while riding in a car, you pass a small white dog with black patches this is said to be a warning of impending vehicular problems.

For a strange small black dog to make three or seven circles on your lawn is believed an omen that a member of your family is in imminent danger.

Seeing a dog and fox playing together is a sign of better times ahead.

To see a large tan dog with a black face carrying a dead white rabbit is said to omen war.

Sighting a dog carrying a dead weasel in its mouth is indicative of a desirable change of weather.

If you are ill or hospitalized and dream of a St. Bernard licking your face, this is regarded as a sure sign you will recover.

Dogwood tree

In the Americas, for your Dogwood to fail to produce blooms is a sign you have dishonored your neighborhood in some manner.

If you are a parent and your Dogwood gets blight it is said you have unfairly caused one of your children emotional anguish.

An expectant mother wishing to find out the gender of her baby is advised to go outdoors and walk beneath the boughs of Dogwoods, as the color of the first flower she finds underneath one will reveal the child's sex: a blue flower or a white with blue shades indicates a boy, while a reddish, pink, purple or yellow flower indicates a girl.

It is common belief that to cut down a Dogwood while you are angry will bring heartache before the next spring. Similarly, cutting down a perfectly healthy Dogwood to make room for anything else brings the offender quick and fitting retribution from the earth spirits.

Finally, to pour a libation of wine mixed with milk (any kind) on the roots of a Dogwood three days in succession will bring one the gift of prophecy. To keep this gift from disappearing, one must repeat the libation every spring.

Door
Some people practice the habit of when visiting a friend or relative, not to leave from the same door they entered, as that by doing so any negative vibrations that came in with them will also leave with them.

Dragon
Seeing a red dragon either in a dream or in the flames of a candle or other fire denotes the impending birth of a renowned person. If the dragon you see is white, however, this means that someone of great fame is about to die.

Seeing a real dragon flying in the sky is said a presage of war for the nation. The exception to this is if the dragon is gold-toned, which is a warning of tribulations solely for the respective community from where the dragon is observed.

Drones (man-made surveillance drones)

To see a drone crash into a tree is a sign of good fortune for the community.

To glimpse a drone flying from over your shoulder augurs that false rumors are afoot.

For a drone to collide into a barn or other structure on a farm signifies the farmer will know prosperity after a period of hard times.

It is considered bad luck if you see a drone in flight and utter a wish - lest the wish you're making is for someone deserving of misfortune, for the very opposite will be granted to the offending party.

Drowsiness (sudden, inexplicable)

Overpowering drowsiness, which is not caused by exhaustion, sleep deprivation, alcohol consumption, drugs or pregnancy, is often cited as the body's call to sleep and heal itself.

Ducklings

Give the name *George* to the first duckling you see in spring to insure a carefree season.

If a dark duckling unexpectedly swims up while you're swimming outdoors, it is believed you will avoid catching a cold for the rest of the season.

Eagles

Throughout recorded history, the eagle has often been regarded as a messenger of the gods and a deliverer of communications from those who have passed on. Human beings still have an awe and reverence for this majestic bird, and certain beliefs surrounding eagles survive in our modern culture. Some of these include:

Eagles guide courageous souls into the afterlife.

To see an eagle pursuing a turkey vulture is a sign your troubles are near an end.

For an eagle to drop prey near your feet is a warning your shameful behavior has been duly noted by the ancestors.

If you find eagle feathers, never keep them in a cellar or basement as this may be considered an insult to the spirit of this soaring bird. Rather, keep the feathers in the highest part of your dwelling to show respect for the eagle's role as a divine messenger.

Intentionally killing an eagle is generally considered to bring bad luck.

In the United States, many people have an image of the American Bald Eagle displayed prominently in their home as a symbol of their patriotism. Likewise, giving one's child a toy or plush American Eagle is thought to petition the bird to redeem the family of any unpatriotic transgressions committed by one of them. And to carry a piece of bone that has been carved or otherwise imprinted with an American Bald Eagle is said to bring about liberation from domineering people.

Ears
There are some curious superstitions regarding ears, which more often than not have nothing to do with hearing. Among these is the supposition that people with dangling lobes (earlobes not attached to the head) tend to be vivacious but prone to lying.

Another belief is that those born with ears that don't match have a distinct cruel streak in their nature.

Men with large ears are said to be energetic but clumsy lovers. Women who have large ears are said to be romantically fickle.

Ears that noticeably stick out from the head are thought to indicate a person with an inquisitive nature, but one who can keep a secret.

Small but well-defined ears are said to belong to people who are especially sensitive and/or artistically inclined.

Malformed ears, especially where the top portion is noticeably short and squarish in appearance, are called criminal ears. If such ears are particularly small and thick, the person is also said to be prone to acts of violence.

Love of money is attributed to those who possess hairy earlobes.

People with natural clefts or deep wrinkles in their earlobe(s) are thought to suffer inherent heart conditions.

An old but still popular belief is that if your ears burn it means someone is talking about you.

EBay
The chance winning of a bid at EBay is said to be aided if the bidder keeps marigold petals close by.

Some claim that you can change a customer's negative review at EBay by performing an act of kindness for an elderly stranger.

Eggs
To drop a fresh egg and break it ushers in minor aggravations, but these can be avoided by immediately giving your left shoulder a light slap.

Finding a piece of pineapple in your egg drop soup is said to usher in 33 days of good luck.

Discovering your egg is double-yoked is thought to be bring general good luck into your daily affairs.

Engagement ring

A woman who loses her engagement ring in a swimming pool is thought to be having second thoughts about marriage.

Dire consequences are said to await the man who gives a woman an engagement ring that has been returned to him by another.

If your hair gets ensnared on your engagement ring, some jealous soul is wishing the worst for your relationship.

If your engagement ring fits over your knuckle yet frequently spins or turns on the finger, it is said you will receive plenty of wild rides in the marriage bed.

Envelopes
If you cut your tongue while licking an envelope, expect a surprising response from your recipient.

Receiving a letter with a yellowish or beige colored smudge on the left corner of the envelop omens the sender or someone in their family is very ill.

Eyewear
To find a dried soapy droplet on your contact lens is warning someone is trying to fool you.

For an ant to run across your glasses while you are wearing them means you will soon be rushed for time.

For a leaf of grass, seed or other piece of vegetation to get wedged in the hinge of your glasses denotes you have forgotten something on your schedule.

If you wish to attract the love of a highly intelligent person, obtain a discarded pair of prescription glasses and clean them first with vinegar, and secondly with water. Find a vase and write your name on the bottom. Place pink carnations in the vase, and set both the glasses and the flowers in a place where moonlight will fall on them. Encircle both vase and glasses with a green string or cord and leave undisturbed for three nights. After this time, bury the glasses near your place of residence and place the carnations on top of the soil that covers the glasses. Don't visit or look on this location for at least nine days.

There are a few interesting beliefs about the color of plastic-based eyeglass frames going around: Wearers of dark or deep purple plastic-based frames are believed to be talented multi-taskers. Those who choose brown plastic frames are thought to be adventurous in bed. Beige frames denote a wearer who is shy but doesn't want to be. Bright yellow frames are the choice of those looking to be noticed. Pink plastic frame wearers like to have a good time but don't hold their liquor well. Those who wear red plastic frames are thought to be devious by nature. Solid black frames are the choice of people who take themselves too seriously. People who have polka-dot frames are alleged to be consummate social butterflies.

To lose a contact while kissing someone is said to mean you've found the person you are meant to be with.

To remove a contact and discover a yellow smudge on it means you have wisely dodged a bad relationship.

For a hair to get between a contact and your eye tokens that you need to change your plans.

Falcon
For a falcon to alight on the rooftop of a home signifies an argument is or about to take place among the occupants. If the falcon is holding prey in a talon, expect the argument to be very heated.

Falling stars
Making a wish on a falling star is an age-old practice still followed today. For your wish to come true, though, avoid disclosing it to anyone.

At seeing a falling star, shout out the first word (even a name) that comes to your lips. As long as the word comes automatically -without thought- it is supposed to have prognostic meaning for you.

Fat (grease)
For the fat from your meat to spill in your lap and leave an impression in the form of a half-moon, be wary someone is looking to take advantage of you.

If you bite into a pocket of hot fat while eating chicken, a lucrative opportunity is coming your way.

Feet
One commonly shared belief today is that the size of a man's feet is proportional to (or at least reflective of) the length of his penis. Similarly, some think that a woman with small feet has petite genitalia.

High arches and arches that "fall" -a tendon problem- point to an individual with a sensitive nature. People with flat feet are often thought to be more emotionally brusque than others, and to possess an innate physical hardiness.

Those who have very hairy toes are said to be sexually uninhibited. If there is much hair on the top of a person's foot, it is assumed they have problems controlling their temper. If this hair is red, they are thought to be adept burglars as well!

Fitted sheet corners
If your fitted sheet corners are snapping loose, it is an sign from Aphrodite that the owner of the bed is becoming a lazy lover.

Flea market
To argue over the asking price of a tee shirt at a flea market is said to denote a miserly nature.

If you find something you have long sought at a flea market, it is suggested to offer the seller half the price, but if they decline this price, to pay the asking price with a wink, lest your purchase turn regrettable.

To sell kites at a flea market is said to attract lightning and thunderstorms.

Fonts
Don't email or otherwise contact someone using a font that you personally find unsettling, as this will distort your intentions to whomever receives the message.

Football jersey
Women who lend their friend a jersey once worn by their football playing boyfriend or husband is said to be inviting injury to her man.

Football player
If your aim is to be a successful professional football player, take a little grass or turf from the field where your first winning game was played. Keep the grass or turf in a pig leather pouch and carry this around your neck during your every meal and while you sleep.

Footwear
To break in another person's shoes for them is reputed to bring illness to both you and the owner.

A woman that has a cork wedge heel to break will soon meet a handsome older man.

To realize you've unintentionally put your flip-flops on the wrong feet is a warning that bill collectors are looking for you.

To suffer a flea bite while wearing flip-flops is a warning not to visit a stranger's home.

To wear gold shoes to a friend's wedding denotes you do not highly value the friendship.

If you take off a boot and find your initials written out in dust or mud on one of them is a sign that someone misses you.

To find a honey bee in your shoe is thought to be a sign that prosperity is on the way.

To go to church wearing sneakers with bright green laces will lead you to doubt or question your religion.

Avoid walking into a fire station wearing orange shoes, as this is said to make people unreasonably suspicious of you.

To find a tack in the sole of your shoe is a sign from the gods you have recently escaped some unrealized danger.

For a bride seeking ecstasy on her wedding night, it is suggested she wear silk shoes during the ceremony.

Wearing brocade slippers is said to attract sensual interest to you.

Write your name along with that of your lover on the rubber of your left sneaker to make your relationship invulnerable to family objections.

Never wear a pair of plaid socks with red seams while boarding a train as this is believed to bring woe to all the passengers.

If while trying to untie your laces new knots accidentally form, you will soon have reason to walk outside again.
(See also Velcro (closures))

Forehead
It is widely held that if the center of your forehead (third eye area) stings or burns it means someone is trying to force their will over you.

Fortune cookies
If you would have your fortune from a cookie come true, you must eat at least one nibble of the cookie.

To open your fortune cookie before the meal has been eaten is said to negate the fortune.

Freckles

Babies born with freckles are thought to be destined to grow up and be very successful for their bold and/or innovative ideas.

Anyone with a freckle or freckles on their earlobes are thought to be uncannily adept at solving mysteries.

Having freckles over your upper lip indicates you have all it takes to be an impressive orator.

Someone with a patch of freckles on the hip just above the buttocks is rumored to be a true master or mistress of amorous play.

Fresh water mussels

To prepare a homemade pasta dinner using local ingredients will prove disappointing if foreign mussels are added to the sauce, as it is believed foreign mussels are antagonistic to regional flavors.

A woman who seasons an already prepared meal of fresh water mussels with more than one seasoning strengthens her chance of one day giving birth to twins or triplets.

To mix fresh water mussels with sea mussels is said to cause nightmares.

Eating yogurt with fresh water mussels is said to make one lazy.

Possessing a pearl from a Norwegian fjord mussel is said to increase one's defenses against arthritis.

To find a Tennessee River pearl is said to bring you the blessings of feminine earth and water spirits. To wear Tennessee River pearls as earrings enhances a person's natural intuitive powers. To wear them as pendants is said to help you develop financial shrewdness.

To flush freshwater mussels down a toilet invites floods.

Fried chicken
To partake of fried chicken without some kind of potato dish is said to bring bad luck.

Eating fried chicken with white gravy is thought to draw general good luck. If the meal is taken on a Sunday, you will soon make new friends.

For an adult to peel off the coating of their fried chicken prior eating it is considered an insult to the gods of cooking, and ushers in a host of small aggravations!

Friend's name
If you catch yourself mistakenly addressing a friend by another friend's name, make a X sign over your heart at once lest both friends forget or neglect you entirely.

If you see a friend's full name appear in the credits of a movie, rap your elbow three times so your friend will always receive deserving credit for their good works.

Frogs
If a bullfrog eating a toad crosses your path, this is a warning that a debt collector is looking for you.

Finding a frog among your Four O'clock's is a sign that a lengthy bout of dry, hot weather is on the way.

Some say that to see a frog sitting on the windshield of a car is a sign rain is coming.
For your path to be crossed by a line of frogs is thought to mean a flood or deluge is imminent.

Frozen treat sticks (wooden)
A stack of these placed nine high and set in the kitchen window is thought to entice the favor of friendly house spirits.

Garbage bags

To keep unwanted pests away from your premises, it is advised to use the last two garbage bags from a dispenser at the same time.

Gems and precious stones
To maintain healthy teeth and gums, some people wear a piece of white jade stone carved in the shape of an apple.

Some maintain that for a woman to wear more than one piece of turquoise jewelry will bring them trouble from the spirit world. But for men, the wearing of multiple turquoise pieces is thought to encourage spiritual understanding.

Fairy stones (aka fairy crosses), are said to be the tears of fairies that fell to the ground when Christ died, and jewelry made of them are popular with those of the Christian faith. However, it is also thought the fairy folk will reclaim these stones if left unattended; so it is suggested that when not wearing your fairy stone or cross you should keep them in a container either made of iron or one that has an iron clasp.

Jewelry set with Tiger's Eye stones are believed to attract friendship to the wearer.

Some put faith in the belief that to wear a belly ring set with a piece of amber will keep the wearer from unwanted sexual harassment.

Possessing a black pearl is thought to stimulate literary interest and goals.

People born under the sign of Cancer are warned to never wear sapphires else they will suffer depression.

Quartz crystals affixed to a pair of sandals are said to enhance the wearer's skill at astral projection.

A red garnet placed near the heart is thought to make the wearer nostalgic. To sew this gem onto your socks or a pair of stockings will lead you to a reunion with an old friend. Wearing a tiara or barrettes set with garnet is said to grant one the aura of nobility.

Wearing a belt buckle set with a bloodstone is said to keep you from intoxication.

Taking a bath with a hematite in the tub is suggested for drawing out illnesses.
Prior to the bath, polish the hematite with a cotton cloth (dispose of the cotton cloth before entering the water). After the bath, be sure to rinse the hematite with clean water and allow it to dry in the sunshine before using again.

To wear a black diamond will open your eyes to false lovers.

Gingers (natural redheads)
The contemporary assertion that gingers have no soul can be blamed (in probably no small part) to an episode from the popular Comedy Central cartoon series, *South Park.* As obviously fictional as the assertion is, the idea is rumored to have a strong belief base among younger viewers.

Globes
If you believe in reincarnation and desire to know where you lived in one of your past lives, consult a class-room style globe in the following manner: Give the globe three gentle spins. Before the globe comes to a stop, close your eyes and with the tip of your forefinger touch the globe. Now open your eyes. Wherever in the world you see your fingertip touching, be assured that you once lived there or passed through during another lifetime.

Golf course
To see an alligator cross a golf course means severe rains are on the way.

Graduation
For an owl to visit a graduation is said to omen the premature demise of the Valedictorian.

Not tossing your cap at the end of a graduation ceremony will bring you difficulty in finding a lucrative job.

It is said that to wear a pin-stripe suit under your graduation gown tokens you will squander your degree by turning to a life of crime.

To win independence from any circumstances holding you back, hang the tassel from your graduation cap from the rear-view mirror of your vehicle.

Graffiti

By bringing into your home or room a piece of outdoor graffiti, you invite the vibrations from the artist's personality in as well.

A graffiti artist's message, if drawn in white and bordered in black, is said to live on long after the artist's death.

Graffiti of red letters bordered by black are thought to be inspired by evil unearthly forces.

Graffiti penned by blue ink and found on a restroom door or wall is believed to be the work of a fickle mind. In contrast, restroom graffiti done in red ink is supposed to be the work of a serious individual.

Restroom graffiti that is a religious quote is considered the work of a lunatic desperate for followers.

Gum

It is a common belief that anyone who carries an unopened pack of chewing gum in their pocket is easily tempted to take up illicit vices.

If someone nearby bursts their bubblegum you should say, "Around the world in 80 days!" to prevent the gum from gluing to the blower's hair.

Gumbo

To spill gumbo while serving it to another is a warning that you are typically known for your stinginess.

To accidentally drop an unintended ingredient in a pot of gumbo means you will have more guests than expected.

If you intended to add some liquor to your gumbo but forgot it, take it as divine intervention because the priest or minister will be dropping by.

Hair buns
If your hair is pinned up in a bun while you are getting a mugshot, expect further legal troubles within the year.

Hairdressers
It is said to be unwise to tip a hairdresser in change. *(See also Tipping)*

Some believe that to insure a good cut by the hairdresser, they should snip the ends off one of their head hairs before arriving to the salon.

Hammer
To find an abandoned hammer is a generally good omen.

A woman who wants to know if she is able to get pregnant is advised to pick up a sturdy metal hammer and turn the handle skyward. If the bracelet she wears can slide down the handle to the hammer and make a pleasing sound, she is said to be fertile. If, however, the bracelet fails to make any sound on striking the hammer, the woman is probably past her child-bearing years.

If someone causes you mental anguish, write their name on a slip of paper, then beat it thirteen times with a hammer. Bury the slip of paper and spit on the earth covering it. This is thought to break the other person's influence over you without resorting to actual violence.

Hangers (clothes hangers)

Drop a clothes hanger and your day will be filled with more acts of clumsiness unless you immediately smack the hanger across your right palm.

Head, Neck, Hair and Scalp
It is considered an ill-omen to bump your head while getting into a car you are thinking about buying or renting.

For a win while gambling, many women believe rubbing the dome of a bald man brings good luck.

If you feel the nape of your neck burn without apparent cause, it is said that an ex-lover is gossiping about you.

To find your beloved has left a hickey on your temple indicates they will speak well of you in the afterlife.

Finding a spider in your hair means you will not die of starvation.

If you unexpectedly find a louse (head lice) in your hair or on your person, burn it immediately in a flame to hinder more from finding you.

To keep a lover thoughtful about texting you, wrap or tie one of their hairs around your cell phone or texting device.

In order to stay aware of your children's activities, it is recommended to place one of your eyebrow hairs inside the case of their pillow.

If your neck throbs in the midst of a thunderstorm, expect to soon meet up with wet company.

To avoid detection of cheating while at school, place a single grape Nerds candy between your ear and scalp.

Heavy perspiration (naturally heavy sweaters)
People who perspire easily and heavily are thought ones who find it difficult to either lie or to keep a secret. It is also perceived these individuals have short tempers, but hate to put on

pretenses. Although their personalities are sometimes said to be overbearing, they are also credited with outgoing dispositions and to be typically optimistic.

To offer confections or honey to a heavy sweater is believed to make the rest of your week just as sweet.

To be offered coffee by a heavy sweater is believed to inspire in you problem-solving ideas.

Homework
It is said you can get a good grade on any homework if, before being turned in, it has been passed between the thighs of a black-haired woman with a beauty mark on her left cheek.

Writing the name *Alice Cooper* in the bottom left-hand corner on the back of your homework is believed to bring about an unscheduled school break.

One's homework is thought safe from theft or copy by kissing a puppy and then immediately kissing the homework page(s).

Homeless people
To harass, mock or offer any kind of cruelty to a homeless Veteran invites problems with your reproductive system.

To indifferently pass by a blind beggar brings scandal into your life. This can be alleviated by returning to the beggar, asking for their forgiveness and leaving them with a ten-dollar bill.

If you steal from a homeless person you will soon be robbed yourself.

Honey
Throughout the centuries, this food created by the bees has been revered by many cultures for its purity and healing qualities. It was consumed by the ancient Egyptians in the belief it aided in longevity, and used in contemporary times to heal burns and to stave off infections.

Today, the consumption of honey is is assumed by some to purify words. It is also believed to make palatable harsh words and phrases to the ears of one's listeners. It is for this reason some politicians allegedly sip honey before giving a speech.

Honeybee
To accidentally swallow a honeybee that has flown into a drink or onto food is said to mean there is at least one French ancestor perched somewhere in the boughs of your family tree.

Hosiery
(See Pantyhose and Stockings)

Hot Dog
If you are invited to a grill-out and receive a hot dog with nicely seared lines is said to denote you are well thought of by the one who grilled it.

To order a grilled dog at a restaurant and find it has no sears denotes your willpower will be soon tested.

Household batteries
Dropping a battery while trying to place it where it's needed means you will soon encounter frustrating people.

To fall because you've stumbled over a battery is a sign that a well-laid plan will go awry.

To find, in an unexpected place, an unopened pack of batteries not past their expiration date means you have made the right choice in a recent important matter.

Internet (see also Media works)
The world-wide web and every technological advance it's bred has created a very unique global folklore. Among the countless superstitions surrounding internet/online use:
For every emoji you use, you lose one brain cell.

To cure anyone suffering from warts or acne, *Rickroll* them.

Many people attest that giving a *Like* and *Share* and/or comment with "Amen" to a posted photo of money brings amazingly fast monetary rewards.

To successfully banish evil spirits or other troubling otherworldly entities from your home, it is advised to view a Weird Al video at 3:33 AM for three mornings in a row. To summon demons, start watching Justin Bieber videos at 6:39 AM.

Women wanting long, luxurious hair are recommend to watch videos of golden retrievers while eating the marrow of bones.

To protect a computer from viruses and other nasties, some people keep a fresh daisy near their computer or laptop while online. Similarly, to stand near burgeoning daisies while using your cell phone is said to keep the connection clear and to prevent dropped calls.

The eating of corn flakes shortly before retiring to bed is rumored to help alleviate internet addiction..

To make and upload to the internet a video of somebody being pranked, be sure to have their permission - otherwise, you can expect to be the butt of pranks three times over!

If someone emails you a curse or chain letter, you can defeat potential danger by immediately reciting every character name you can remember from the movie *Goonies.*

According to some former enthusiasts, headaches, eye strain and other maladies caused by too much computer activity can be eased by soaking one's palms in ice water for twenty minutes and staying off the computer or device for at least forty-eight hours.

Reciting the Lord's Prayer is said to keep one uninterested in watching online porn.

Wearing a Thor's Hammer is thought to ward off all desires to start or participate in online flaming.

One charm alleged to cure baldness: 48-72 hours before the moon turns full, type the term *woolly mammoth* into your search engine. Print out the first picture of a woolly mammoth the search brings up. Place this picture under your bed for nine days. Bury the picture outside under moss. According to the theory, your hair should begin growing in thick and luxurious within the coming lunar month.

To keep one's partner from online cheating, secretly place a box of chocolates, along with a photograph of yourself under the place they sleep.

To be gifted with the ability to spot lucrative financial investments, speak the name *Steve Jobs* five times -no more, no less- in front of a mirror.

Owning a black cat is considered a ward against computer gremlins. However, to mistreat a black cat is will bring you the harassment of computer gremlins.

If you visit a webpage and are subjected to hearing a video you didn't select to play, you can curse the webmaster with three months of business woes by saying the name *Bill Gates* three times in succession.

To read three media stories in a row about the Kardashian family is said to bring a natural disaster wherever you reside in the world.

To speak disparagingly of Lady Diana while checking your online horoscope is reputed to shorten your life.

To accidentally hit play on a video showing cute babies, you are guaranteed a sunny future.

To inadvertently come across nude images of your favorite celebrity, you will soon be obligated to eat something you don't like.

If you purposely fake negative reviews on a classic rock-in-roll video, you will lose your hearing in one ear.

To post a review of a book you actually have not read is said to incur divine justice from the spirit of Edgar Allen Poe.

If you flirt with your friend's significant other or spouse online, and deny it to them when confronted, you will give birth to idiot children and die in poverty.

If you troll you will be trolled.

To check your Twitter status while driving brings about incurable acne.

To refer to someone as Bae online condemns you to a loss of IQ points.

To knowingly pass Spam will make you fat and thirsty.

If you set up a FundMe-type page in the hopes of avoiding work, it is said you will end up with more children than you can afford.

To make a cruel comment about the mugshot of a dead person is reported to bring demons to your household.

To forward a Nigerian spam email will make you go mad. To intentionally send someone a computer virus will cause hair to grow on your tongue and your vision to fail.

If someone has declared a spoiler alert warning on their post or thread and you complain about their spoiler anyway, your property will be defecated on by wild animals.

If you unintentionally capture someone dying while taking a selfie, you will gain seven years of natural life. On the other hand, if you stage such a picture, you will be haunted by angry spirits. And, if you are unintentionally photographed committing a crime in another person's selfie, you will be plagued by halitosis.

Avoid giving a LIKE to a post or picture if you really don't like it, as a bogus or meaningless LIKE brings retaliation from computer gremlins.

Irises
This iconic flower is believed to attract angels, elves, fairies, pixies and other magical folk if sewn around the home. Not only this, bumblebees love them.

Pictures of blue irises hung on office walls imbue the atmosphere with clear thinking and general positive relations in the work area. Blouses and shirts with blue iris prints help lift the wearer's outlook on life. Donning clothes bearing images of orange or peach colored irises is thought to keep one energetic during shopping trips.

Yellow irises and images of them are said to help the healing process, which may be why pictures of them are often hung on hospital walls.

Irish twins
Siblings born of the same parents and within the same year are called Irish twins. This quaint term did not come about from quaint sources, but rather originated from bigots who used the Irish custom of having large families as another excuse to stereotype them. Despite its racist beginnings, the term Irish twins is today seen as a badge of honor for those who have been blessed with two children born within twelve months of each other. All the same, certain beliefs regarding Irish twins do exist:

Irish twins are thought to be more apt to feel jealousy toward one another than toward any of their other siblings.

It is believed Irish twins will spar hardest for the affections of their parents.

If one Irish twin is favored over the other, the disfavored one will work hardest to succeed in life.

Irish twins will argue the most with parents, but by the same token, race to their parents' defense before anyone else.

An older sister who has doted on Irish twin siblings has a reserved seat of honor in heaven.

Jelly Beans
Finding a brown jelly bean in a bag of ordinary ones means you are watched over by Ostara, the Germanic goddess of fertility.

Jimi Hendrix
Among rock connoisseurs it is believed that to compare hip hop or pop stars to the great guitarist Jimi Hendrix provokes the wrath of the Rock gods and will bring divine retribution. If you discover you've committed this error, immediately point heavenward with a forefinger and say, "Experience!" and you will be absolved.

Job interview
It is said that the wearing of bright yellow colors to an interview will make the interviewer dubious of your experience.

To wear white shoes to a job interview is not advised as this color at the ankles is thought to be distracting.

Some believe that carrying a small piece of coal or an acorn during an interview promotes your chances of landing the job.

Coming to an interview with grungy teeth is thought to work against your chances of employment.

If you are being interviewed for the position of exotic dancer, wearing a perfume or oil containing lily of the valley or orris root is thought to improve your chances of getting hired.

Keys
To lose and then discover your car key while at the beach is said to bring you new friends and acquaintances.

To discover your house key is bent without explanation indicates you have aroused the ire of unfriendly spirits.

To find a mysterious key in your attic that fails to fit any of the locks in your home, augurs that you will soon find treasure.

To find a diary key that doesn't belong to you or anyone you know indicates that fame will be someday be thrust upon you.

If you come across an old whiskey bottle with a key in it, you can expect to live to a ripe old age.

Knees
If you feel a tickling twinge in both knees this is supposed to mean you will soon be in the presence of someone who awes you.

To nick your knee while shaving is a warning that a romantic interest wants to pressure you into making a decision you aren't ready for.

Laundry detergent
According to some, if after using the machine you find a portion of unused detergent on top of the agitator, you will soon be making amends for a wrong.

Lawn gnomes
To deliberately knock over a lawn gnome is said to bring you a year of bad luck.   To pick up a knocked-over lawn gnome and set it right is thought to bring you compassion when most needed.

Lawyers (see attorneys)

Lemon drops (candy)
Lemon drops that have been stored in a windowsill where they will catch the rays of the sun are thought to have a healthy energizing effect on whoever eats one.

Lighters (and matches)

If a friend tells you that your lighter showed up in their home, let them keep it as it was meant to be there. If a friend returns a lighter you lost, it means the two of you will having a lasting relationship.

Never purchase a white disposable lighter as it will bring misfortune. However, if you are offered a light from a white disposable, it augurs you will have peaceful dreams.

Carrying in your shirt pocket a lighter with a gecko or lizard on it is said to help develop one's sense of humor.

A man who offers a woman a light for her cigarette without being asked will be blessed with long-lasting sexual endurance.

A woman who steals a man's lighter to light a candle, then returns the lighter to him without being noticed will always have many friends.

If you strike a flame from a wet match it is said you have been gifted with the ability to see the future.

Finding a pack of matches that smell of a lady's perfume denotes you will soon have a windfall at gambling.

To light a match off a burning cigar is thought to usher in bad weather.

To successfully strike a match on your denim pants will bring you gain through real estate. To successfully strike a match on a friend's denim will bring newcomers into your circle.

If you find in your kitchen drawer a pack of old matches that don't belong to you it is said you will rise above future adversity.

Lightning
A well-known adage states lightning never strikes twice. While this is generally accepted as a fact of life, there have been a handful of cases where an individual has been struck by

lightning more than once. The reason for their misfortune is accredited to a variety of reasons, such as the rationale that the victim's genetic make-up simple attracts electrical energy. Other speculations include such scenarios as the lightning victim has incurred the wrath of a deity, or by contrast, the strikes are signs of favor from a deity.

Anyone that curses lightning invites catastrophe to their village or town.

Making love outdoors while lightning cracks through the heavens is believed to make hardy children.

Limes

According to some, eating a lime outdoors and spitting the seeds on the ground will change the course of the weather.

Dreaming of eating limes is said to be an omen of impending good fortune.

Wearing clothing with images of limes are supposed to lift one's spirits.

Smelling the fragrance of limes when none are around means friendly spirits are watching over you.

Lions

Having one's thigh or hip brushed by the tail of a passing lion is supposed to instill courage in a mousy individual. (*Caution - never put yourself in danger to test this superstition!*)

Lottery tickets

It is said to augur well to buy a random lottery ticket that has the month, date and second two digits of your birth year among the numbers. However, to selectively purchase a lottery ticket with these numbers is believed to be a fruitless endeavor.

Lucky apparel

Most of us have what we call our "lucky shirt" or "lucky shoes", so it is not surprising there are some superstitions regarding fortunate apparel:

Never wash your lucky pants or shirt with any article of clothing you particularly dislike, or the luck will be worn off.

A lucky pair of undergarments is said to gain even more luck by removing them from the drawer with your teeth!

If your lucky apparel must be sent to a professional cleaner, choosing an honest cleaner that is undergoing hard times is said to triple your luck, and as well rub off freely onto the cleaner. However, if your cleaner behaves unprofessionally, rudely or is untrustworthy, the luck that would be shared with them is said to come with karmic repercussions..

The losing of a lucky garment at a public laundry is probably not a bad thing, as it is believed that in such circumstances the gods have deemed the person finding the garment is in more need of good luck than the original owner.

If you have lost a tie, repeat the following three times, "John Babbacome Lee, please have mercy on me!" By doing this not only will the tie return, but it will henceforth be your lucky one. (John Babbacome Lee was an Englishman, sentenced to hang for the crime of murder. However, after three failed attempts to execute him in this manner, Mr. Lee's sentence was commuted to life in prison. Some years later he walked out of prison a free man. Today, Lee is seen as a sort of patron saint for those struggling with neck wear.)

M&M's® (candies)
It has long been held that anyone who unintentionally draws a green M&M from an offered bag or bowl means are very *amorous*. This belief is still widely regarded as true.

Martin Luther King
Pictures of this inspiring civil rights leader are said to encourage harmony and feelings of brotherhood wherever they are hung.

Reading and/or reciting King's *I have a dream* speech inspires courage in one's self and faith in their fellow man.

Mechanical bull
It is common belief that a woman who gets doused with someone's drink while riding a mechanical bull will soon learn she is to be a mother.

Media works (newspaper, magazines, online sources)
Among news reporters, to utter the name "Jimmy Olsen" (of *Superman* fame) is believed to draw annoying new co-workers.

If you are a newspaper delivery person and deliver the paper to the wrong residence three days in a row, it is said you will soon be related to the family by a marriage. If you are already related to the family, a birth is imminent.

In Scandinavia, for a reporter to purposely misquote a good and upright person is said to incur the displeasure of the god Bragi, and you will be punished with the inability to finish projects.

It is warned that to use visual graphics you know are reported to cause seizures in some individuals, you will develop epilepsy within five years.

Among younger people, it is believed that seeing tedious mention of the name Beyoncé in online news sources will make a man sterile.Likewise, if you post an article about Justin Bieber on somebody's FB page without permission, that person will be the cause for your next frustration.

It is an old belief that if while reading the Obituaries you find a deceased bearing your name, or if your own death is falsely reported, ten years is added to your life. A more recent belief alleges that to see someone sharing your name in an online celebrity arrest story brings you a broken bone for each mention of the name in the article.

To falsely report a UFO sighting to any media source brings you to the attention of real extraterrestrials.

Men in black
Almost everyone has heard of the legendary men in black. Just in case you don't know about them, these guys with in their dark trench coats and sunglasses are said to frequently appear to those who have witnessed sightings of unidentified flying objects (UFO's). What may be lesser known is that some people believe that just obsessing on or talking often about the men in black can make them show up at your doorstep. So guard your tongue and hold the enthusiast interest in check!

Microwave ovens
There are a few superstitions about this staple of modern kitchen appliances:

To find a live bug in the microwave while taking food out means a relative is hiding something from you.

If you set the timer properly and carefully watch over the heating process, yet your popcorn still comes out scorched, someone you know is in danger of losing their job.

If your timer throws up words instead of numbers, or if the numerals flash on and off in a crazy manner, your house is said to be under the scrutiny of extraterrestrials.

For a potato to squeal in the microwave is a sign that an elderly relative waits to be visited.

Trickster ghosts are alleged to open and slam shut microwave oven doors for the sheer fun of harassing the living.

If the timer bell keeps going off after being disabled or turned off is a sign you have offended benevolent elementals.

Mission Impossible (theme music)
A popular belief surrounding this piece by composer Lalo Schifrin maintains that listening to it while making love will

enhance a man's performance and make a woman very adventurous!

Mistletoe
Still common is the tradition of couples kissing under the Yuletide mistletoe. To kiss a pregnant woman (that is not your lover or spouse) beneath mistletoe is said to keep one from enduring hardship for the duration of winter.

Seeing a white hound with milky eyes standing under mistletoe is purported to mean somebody you care about is battling a life-threatening illness.

Conceiving a child under mistletoe is said to guarantee the child will grow up to possess sage-like wisdom.

As mistletoe was the weapon which the treacherous Loki used to kill Baldur, this parasitic plant is also seen as a symbol of betrayal. For mistletoe to fall on you denotes treachery is afoot.

Monopoly (the board game)
Monopoly has been one of the bestselling board games of all time (perhaps the bestselling board game of all time!), and several superstitions surrounding the game have evolved: Carrying in your shoe the *Get out of jail free* card while driving will get you out of any speeding ticket with just a warning.

If your token is the dog and you own both Park Place and Boardwalk but still manage to lose the game, expect to be *treated like a dog* within the next 24 hours.

Anyone who has won a game of Monopoly using the top hat token and then places the token in their wallet will be irresistible to women.

If you cause an opponent to go bankrupt because they owe you utility rent, be prepared to go hungry all the next day.

Any player who snatches up both Park Place and Boardwalk by landing on each with a roll of snake eyes (1 pip side of each dice), they are said to be favored by the devil. Additionally, if this player happens to be the banker in the game it is said they are doomed to die a wealthy but lonely skinflint.

According to legend, you can expect the loss of a romantic interest if you pick the Community Chest's *You have won second prize in a beauty contest!* card three times during the course of a single game.

Moths
To come across a dead white moth captured in a spider's web is a warning someone outside of your family is speaking ill of a deceased loved one.

Movie Theater
Movie theaters have been around for many decades, and subsequently several superstitions regarding these arenas have developed:

Eating popcorn in a theater without spilling a single one is said to augur prosperous times ahead.

An unexpected pregnancy is allegedly in the horizon for a women who experiences the unpleasant situation of sitting in a theater seat soaked by urine.

To be harassed by a buzzing fly while watching the movie means annoying news awaits at home. If the harassing insect is a moth, expect sad news from a neighbor or relative. *(See also Moths)*

Agreeing to go on a date with an usher is ill-advised if this is the first time the two of you have met.

Rapping your knuckles lightly on the snack/candy counter is said to bring an unexpected monetary refund in the near future. Speaking impatiently to the vendor is ill-advised as it is believed to bring the offender accidents on the way home.

If you enjoy the movie, it is said that keeping the theater ticket stub in your wallet will bring you in contact with pleasant and interesting people. If, however, the movie was disappointing, it is recommended to discard the stub asap to avoid negative people coming into your life.

Finding the name Jimmy Stewart written in gold-colored ink on a theater's restroom door is a sign your guardian angel is diligently doing their job.

Discovering a tissue clinging to your shoe while walking through a movie theater aisle is said to augur you will be popular in unpopular crowds.

Being loudly chatty or otherwise distracting while the movie is showing is supposed to insure you will be plagued with a poor night's sleep.

A week filled with inconveniences is said to be the punishment for those who intentionally blurt out the film's ending to those waiting for the next showing.

Because of a tragic recent event, it is believed by many that neither the name of actor Heath Ledger nor the character name *the Joker* should be spoken in a dark movie theater.

Muffin top (a protruding female mid-drift)
If your muffin top causes a button to pop off your blouse, it is believed you will soon become acquainted with a heavy-set man.

If a puppy falls asleep on top of your muffin top, expect a family member to soon be cradling a new addition to their family.

Names
To wed someone that shares your last name, the marriage will last no longer than the courtship.

If at the beach you find what appears to be your name written out in the swirls of the sand denotes you will be visited by from someone you have not seen in a long time.

Narwhal tusk
Impotency in men is said curable if they carry or wear a piece of narwhal tusk (tooth). Similarly, a man will have more sexual stamina during lovemaking if the headboard is carved with an image of a narwhal.

Necklace clasps
To safeguard your friendships, if while wearing a necklace you discover the clasp has moved to the front of your throat or chest, kiss it and return it to the back.

If the clasp of your pearl necklace breaks and the pearls fall to the floor or ground, it denotes someone you trust has betrayed you. However, if you gather the pearls with only your bare hands and place them in a crystal vessel for a week, you will soon have new allies.

New Year
There are several popular traditions of the superstitious nature surrounding the New Year:
To partake of freshly made rice pudding along with the celebratory champagne or wine is said to renew fertility (temporarily) in women past their child-bearing years..

In the United States, and particularly the south, to eat black-eyed peas on the first day of the new year is believed to insure a prosperous year ahead.

To entice bright blessings into the home, some place a raw, unpeeled sweet potato on the outside of their front door at the first dawn of the new year.

According to some, people who refuse to sing *Auld Lang Syne* at the entrance of the new year are doomed to know bitterness the whole year through.

It is said that whomever you kiss within the very first minute of the new year will be unable hold a lasting grudge against you for the next twelve months.

If, during the celebration of the new year, you are showered with confetti made of old newspapers, expect to meet up an old friend.

If you conceive within minutes before the new year arrives it is said you will give birth to a child with a wise old soul.

A child born within twenty-four hours before the new year will grow up both clever, responsible and compassionate.

Nickel (coin)
An unmarried person that discovers a nickel in their left shoe can expect to have five serious relationships before meeting the person they are destined to be with. Married individuals finding a nickel in their left shoe can look forward to having either five children, five grandchildren or at least five living descendants when they die.

To find a nickel in your right shoe is a sign you will come into unexpected cash within five days.

A newly minted nickel carried in a pouch is said to bring one in contact with frugal and reliable business associates.

Keeping on your person a nickel which was minted in the year of your birth will open your eyes to scams and untrustworthy opportunists.

Keeping a buffalo head nickel beside your phone is rumored to elicit calls from the dead.

Nose
An itching nose that can't be relieved is said to augur the coming of a visitor.

Ogress of Reading

Amelia Elizabeth Dyer, aka the Ogress of Reading, was a serial murderer of infants in Victorian England. Dyer's victim tally was so prolific that even after more than a century since her execution, her horrific deeds have become the stuff of storytelling legend. These bogeyman tales aside, however, there are many who caution against uttering Dyer's name or her moniker in the confines of any institution that deals with foster care or adoption service. To speak of the Ogress of Reading, it is said, will be taken as an invitation by her unrepentant spirit to come and continue the cold-hearted work she left behind.

Opal
Wearing jewelry set with an opal is generally considered to bring bad luck unless you were born in the month of October or under the astrological sign of Libra.

O'possums
In the United States the term *to play 'possum* means to pretend to be dead until an attacker has gone off. While real o'possums aren't often reported to practice this act of self-defense, they are known for their typically benign behavior, and the female of the species for carrying her young on her back. Out of these habits a few beliefs have circulated:

If you come across a dead female o'possum on the road or beside it, and rescue the live babies from her pouch, it is said you will never know abandonment.

An o'possum skull placed on a mantle or affixed to a wall is believed to bar ghosts and bill collectors from the domain.

A taxidermied o'possum placed on one's front lawn or porch is thought to keep vicious animals off the property.

Hanging pictures or photos of baby o'possums in a nursery or playroom is said to help instill a sense of camaraderie among siblings and friends.

Burying an o'possum paw under one's mail box will soften bad news coming in or leaving out with the mail.

Stand-up comedians are advised to keep hairs of an o'possum on their person so they will avoid the temptation of making unkind jokes.

If a family of o'possums take up residence near your moonshine still, take it as a sign you've picked a good spot to set up your illicit trade.

Showing mercy toward an o'possum will keep enemies or rivals from knowing your business.

To eat from a dish carved or otherwise crafted with an image of an o'possum is said to insure you and yours will eat well come Christmas day.

Palms (interior of hand)
For your left palm to itch suddenly and without explanation means love is coming to you. If it is your right palm with this kind of itch, money is on the way.

Pantyhose and Stockings
Getting a run in pantyhose or stockings is a common irritation, but there is a belief surrounding the number of such tears when they occur to a single pair of hosiery during one wearing: One run means you will be late for an appointment. Two runs means you may expect opposition to an idea. Three or more runs means you will be replaced in somebody's affections.

Piggy bank
It is highly recommended to retrieve your money from a piggy bank without intentionally damaging the bank, otherwise you will face many obstacles replacing the amount. The exception to this rule is if you donate the money to a person in need; as in breaking the piggy bank for a charitable emergency will bring a financial windfall when you are in most need.

Pine needles
Smelling fresh pine needles is believed to cleanse one's thoughts of unnecessary worries and useless clutter.

To get sticky residue on your skin from the handling of pine needles can be difficult to wash off with soap and water. However, to remove the residue in this way, no matter how long it takes, is said to help provide new perspective on a tough situation.

Playground equipment

Violets and/or Sweet William planted at a playground area is supposed to attract the watchful eyes of benevolent fairies. Also, for a child find a Shasta daisy or Sweet William blossom on the equipment, and for which no human hands were seen to place there, means that child is under the protection of fairies.

Pockets

On finding lint in your child's pocket, place it back once the item is washed. This is supposed to keep them honest.

Some contend that to turn a pocket out before washing it will make it easier for money to fall out of it later.

Finding unaccountable money in your own pocket is believed to be a charitable gift from the beyond. To come across three unaccountable pennies in your pocket after washing the garment is an especially good omen.

A lizard found in a pocket is a sign of swiftly changing life events.

To find a hair band in your pocket that is twisted up with hair you don't recognize denotes you will soon be vexed by a female. This annoyance may be avoided by burning both band and hair.

Carrying in your sweater pocket a small egg while on the way to church will make the sermon sweeter to your ears.

The discovery of popcorn in a pocket means you will have a filling dinner.

A broken button found in a pair of trousers is said to signal upcoming family contention.

To cut your hand or finger on a soda pop lid while digging through a pocket means others believe you to be parsimonious..

To pull a red thread out of a white pocket denotes a coming accident. A blue thread found in a red pocket means you have been recognized for your generosity. A blue thread taken from a pink pocket denotes someone close to you is pregnant.

To pull from your pocket a toothpick with an mint or lozenge wrapper attached to it means you are well liked by children.

Pokemon Go
Some players believe that wearing a bright yellow shirt or dress and black socks while playing this game will prevent personal injury.

Postage stamps
To receive a letter with the postage stamp turned upside-down means the sender or their representative will soon be at your door.

To unintentionally apply a postage stamp upside down indicates you will soon have reason to regret what you are mailing.

Pot Pies
This comfort food is a favorite of many, but be aware that to purposely avoid eating the crust of your pot pie is supposed to expose a person with an ungrateful disposition.

It is said when two people unintentionally stick their eating utensils into a pot pie at the same time it is because their destinies have been brought together by higher forces.

Physicians (Doctors)
A physician that forgets the Hippocratic Oath while treating someone is doomed to suffer the same malady, or at least symptoms, as the patient.

(See also Vanity Plates)

Prisms (prismed glass and crystal)
Prismed glass and crystal objects can be very lovely, although there are a few superstitions surrounding their light reflective properties:

Hanging a prismed pendant in a window facing east is said to enhance the morning sun's optimistic presence in the room or dwelling.

For the prism in a piece of jewelry to break is seen as a bad omen of many coming personal trials and hardships. However, your ability to overcome these situations may be had by placing the broken prism (all pieces) in a green or verdant colored pouch and burying this at least six inches in the earth.

One is said able to bring discord to a relationship by wearing prism earrings to a function or event where the couple is in attendance.

It is advised to never set a table piece made of prismed crystal at a wedding, lest you wish arguments to break out among the guests.

To bury a glass or crystal prism in your flower bed is thought to compel the plant into producing particularly abundant blooms, the petals of which will be especially attractive. Likewise, to bury a prism near the roots of a flowering tree is supposed to encourage the tree blooms to be impressive and memorably fragrant.

Prom
If your hair becomes entangled in your friend's prom dress, or vice versa, your friendship will last a long time after graduation.

Wearing orange to your prom will get you easily intoxicated.

Should your corsage fall in the punch, it is said you will be remembered by only a few of your classmates, but among these you will always be cherished.

Fame will find you if you wear black lipstick to the prom and are kissed on the cheek by a red-haired man wearing a white tux.

Wearing a gown of crushed red velvet is said to make you enemies. But a gown of crushed blue will gain you friends.

If your earring falls into a man's punch glass, it is said the two of you will one day wed.

If your tux rips at the prom through no fault of your own, you will soon find your popularity diminishing.

Never leave for the prom in a black limo with red seats lest an accident find you on the route.

For a young man to be asked to dance by his teacher denotes he, too, will someday be a teacher.

Prophecy (gift of)
People who are born of mothers who suffered a gunshot injury during their pregnancy are said to have the gift of predicting the outcome of the Roulette wheel.

If you want the gift of prophecy (and are deserving of it), you can take a barefoot walk in a Louisiana bayou - if you encounter no alligator, snake or other unpleasant beast and come back with no moss or muck on your body, hair or clothing, you are certain to receive the gift.

Individuals who have survived being caught in a tornado's path are thought endowed with better than average hunches about the stock market.

In some areas of the southern United States it is believed that children who enjoy eating rhubarb pie and have the habit of sneaking swigs of moonshine are prophets in the making.

Rabbit
To point at a rabbit you may expect to hear news of a pregnancy, either for yourself, friend or family member.

During the spring the discovery of a rabbit's nest near your front door means you will be faced with a lot of hard work before the Fall.

Wearing rabbit images on pendants or clothing is believed to make one industrious and quick-minded.

Racist (word)
It is believed that to falsely accuse another of being a racist sentences the offender to be similarly accused three times over.

Rain
To be outside and rain begins just as you light a cigarette, expect to hear news or receive an answer you've been waiting for.

If you bump into a pail of rainwater and the water splashes out means someone dear is angry with you.

People who peel tangerines while standing in a downpour are thought to have more confidence than most.

If an oak leaf gets in your hair while it is raining, this is a sign that you will stand strong in a coming confrontation.

Singing *Ave Maria* while walking through the rain is thought to bring general courage.

For the sun to shine while it rains means you should expect more rain to fall the next day and around the same time.

Raisins
To eat of raisins before partaking of wine is believed to strengthen one's resolve to avoid over-indulgence (as long as the wine was made from grapes).

Eating too many chocolate covered raisins is thought to make one drowsy and grumpy.

Some parents offer golden raisins (which come from white grapes) to their offspring in the belief this will brighten the child's disposition.

It is said to give an elderly person a gift of raisins in a wicker basket will draw you soon to hidden treasure.

Ramen noodle soup
It is considered a bad omen to open a packet of ramen noodles and discover the seasoning packet is not there. However, you may change the luck by cooking the noodles and letting them sit until they mold. (Just don't eat the moldy noodles!)

Ravens
Although ravens are members of the crow family, their great size, ruffled neck feathers and solitary habits set them apart from most of their scavenger kin. Their habits have also fascinated human beings for centuries, and in doing so, distinct beliefs regarding ravens have emerged. Unlike crows, ravens are not typically seen as harbingers of Death, but rather recognized as agents and message bearers for the gods themselves.

In our modern times, it is said one may receive wisdom and teachings directly from their deity by meeting the gaze of a raven.

To find a raven's feathers is a rare thing, but if you are so fortunate as to come across one or more outdoors, handle them with reverence. Keeping raven feathers in an oaken container in the central portion of your home is believed to show humility, and also serves to request the presence of your deity to watch over the household.

Burning raven feathers are likewise thought to banish evil spirits, though whoever does this must be sure to offer words of gratitude to the raven for the sacrifice.

Perhaps owing to the popularity of Edgar Allen Poe's gothic masterpiece, *The Raven*, some spiritually intuitive folk believe that to recite the poem during a séance encourages the spirit of Poe to make contact with the participants.

Reading
To read *The Pokey Little Puppy* to an infant while rocking them is believed to instill in the child a love for animals.

If you reach for a cup of tea or coffee while reading and find the handle turned from where you left it means that a dear departed is watching over you.

To use a losing lottery ticket as a bookmark brings untold interruptions while attempting to finish the book.

To use a hawk feather for a bookmark brings victory in the next battle you face.

To write a review of a book before finishing it brings arthritic pain.

Refrigerator door
Many believe that a refrigerator door, uncluttered by photos of loved ones or other memento of some loved one, indicates the owner is unfeeling, a narcissist or both.

Retirement
Some claim that eating some form of oats every morning will insure prosperity after retirement.

RGP gaming
Carrying a small figurine of the wizard *Gandalf* is alleged to bring good luck during the game.

To win a favorable outcome while playing any RGP game about vampires, it is recommended to sleep with a small photograph of actor *Bela Lugosi* under your pillow.

Rhinestones
Attending a funeral while wearing any garment with rhinestones is considered bad luck.

Rhododendrons
This shrub with its showy flowers grows in parts of Asia and also the highlands of Appalachia. It is a hardy plant, noted for thriving in cooler temperatures and once regarded as a favorite by certain gods of ancient cultures. A few superstitions regarding Rhododendrons have remained with us in modern times:

To bury a loved one near Rhododendrons is thought to help the departed to let go of earthly concerns and troubles and facilitate a happy journey into the afterlife.

Sleeping in a field of Rhododendrons is believed to bring one messages from the gods via dreams.

Growing a Rhododendron shrub in front of your home is said to keep one's family emotionally connected and to generally bring heavenly blessings upon the family.

Negotiations between enemies are believed to work out to a satisfactory conclusion for both parties if an uncut and blossoming Rhododendron shrub is brought into the meeting room or area.

Giving a girl or woman a Rhododendron to plant and nurture is thought to keep her from the seduction of unscrupulous men.

Robbery (false claim)
If you claim to have been robbed when you haven't, don't be surprised to be victimized by a real robber within the next three months.

Roosters (images)

Dishes with images of roosters sparring are thought to provoke agitation during a meal. By contrast, dishware with an image of a single rooster is thought to inspire courteous manners among everyone at the table.

To protect your family from disgrace, hang pictures of crowing roosters in the central portion of the home.

Pictures or paintings of cocks protecting hens are thought to grace any humble abode with an atmosphere of nobility.

Hanging an image of a rooster driving a fox away from chicks brings the virtue of loyalty to the occupants of any abode.

Saint Patrick's Day
Many people wear the color green on St. Patrick's Day in honor of the Christian Irish saint and also in recognition of Ireland in general. It has become custom, especially among school-aged children, to pinch any classmate or friend that fails to wear something green on this holiday. There are some that even claim that the failure to not pinch those without green is inviting snakes (snakes, of course, being the creature Saint Patrick is said to have drove out of Ireland).

School bus
Over time, children have entertained a few shared beliefs concerning the riding of school buses. One of these maintains that if the driver forgets to make your to-home stop, their personal vehicle will suffer a flat tire over the coming weekend.

Never ride a bus not assigned to take you home or bad luck will accompany you. However, this warning does not apply if you are riding your friend's bus in order to spend time at their home.

To realize you have dropped or otherwise left a mirror behind on a school bus, this is a warning some teacher or other school official is prying into your affairs.

Doing your homework on the bus ride home is alleged to mean you will lead a very boring adult life.

Finding a drum stick on a school bus is confirmation that you will know future successful following a career path not taught in your school.

Discovering on the bus an old year book means that one day you will be more successful than your parents.

Bad-termpered and/or rude school bus drivers are said to be the by-product of the devil's relationship with a nanny goat.

School meals
If the milk you've been given is past the expiration date, toss it into the garbage from over your left shoulder unless you want a miserable bout of the chicken pox.

Some school children believe that to utter the name *Michelle Obama* while eating a meal at school brings on painful indigestion.

Using a spork to eat meat at school will turn you into a zombie. Additionally, to eat your fruit cup without aid of a spoon will turn you into a useless hippie.

Drawing pictures of literary character *Harry Potter* while eating lunch is thought to help you pass any upcoming test.

Screen door
Screen doors are a fairly modern household item, and a few superstitions about them are known to exist:
To bump or walk into the front screen door while trying to enter an abode indicates you hurt the feelings of someone at the last place you were at. To walk into the front screen door on leaving is a reminder you are about to leave behind something you'll need.

For any part of your apparel to get snagged on a tear in a back screen door on your way out is a warning of precarious events awaiting you in the near future. Getting such a snag on entering through a back screen door is a portent that someone you prefer to avoid is either waiting inside or will arrive soon.

Serial killer (name)
It's believed that any parent who knowingly names their child after a serial killer is automatically penalized with a doubling of their karmic debt.

Shaving cream dispenser
If the shaving cream continues to leak out after you're done with the dispenser, expect an encounter with a petty and bothersome man.

Shoes (See Footwear)

Shopping
For a cordial and happy shopping experience with a friend, never wear a pair of sunglasses that are more expensive than theirs. If this happens unintentionally, be sure to try on theirs while they try on yours.

Skateboards
A depiction of an armadillo on a skateboard is generally regarded as a talisman against injuries while riding. A sketch or drawing of a gecko is thought to boost the speed of one's skateboard.

An image of fireworks or of a one-eyed parrot on a skateboard is thought to beckon distractions for the rider.

To put the name of one's ex on their skateboard draws unseen peril to the skateboarder.

Snake
According to some Native Americans, finding a snake encircled around the roots of a tobacco plant is an auspicious omen that you are being protected by the Creator. Never disturb such a tobacco plant nor molest the snake in any way, just quietly thank the Creator and be on your way.

If you drive over a black snake and kill it can mean one of two things: If done with the deliberate intention of harming the snake, you will have three years of financial loss. To drive over the black snake because you simply couldn't see it or because you were avoiding an accident means you will receive unexpected help and consolation in trying times ahead.

To carry a rattlesnake's rattler while hunting is not advised, for it is believed whatever game you bring home will be sinewy and unpleasant of taste.

Snake skin

To come across a snake skin with the head section pointing away from you means that your enemies are moving away from you. To find one with the head pointing at you or the direction from which you came is a warning enemies still seek you.

Some believe that keeping a snake skin in the glove compartment or trunk of a vehicle will keep the tires safe.

Snipe hunt

In Asia, Europe and New Zealand, snipes are a cute bird known for their long bills and the building of attractive basket-pattern nests. In the United States though, the Snipe is a nocturnal-loving creature of hazy, varying (and typically horrific) physical description, and infamous for its purported aggressive behavior. If you wonder why you've never seen a Snipe at the zoo, remember this: in the southern states and certain other regions of the U.S., it is a tradition among men to set boys out on their first "snipe hunt" as part of a coming-of-age rite. This involves taking the boy outdoors at night -usually in the woods- and posting him at a certain vantage point, alone and with a sack (the only known weapon said to capture the elusive snipe). Of course, once the boy has been sitting long enough by himself in the quiet dark he will begin to hear growls, hoots, hollers and other frightful sounds. If the boy remains all night in wait for his capture, he has passed the test. If he runs screaming for home, the male relatives or friends who set him up enjoy the good laugh they fully expected!

Snow
If you see chickadees looking for food in the snow, feeding them sunflower seeds are believed to help them find warm shelter.

Seeing a solid red cardinal in the snow is thought to be a sign you will have all the necessities to make it comfortably through the rest of winter.

Finding barefoot human footprints in the snow that leads to a wall of your home is said to be a sign that the Nazarene (Christ) is happy with your family.

To keep your romance alive through the winter and beyond, form from the first snow of winter a miniature snow couple. Be sure the couple's hands are clasped and set upon one of them a piece of your clothing or some jewelry and do the same for the other with something that belongs to your beloved. Now carefully place the couple into a freezer. If for any reason your freezer stops working or the snow couple should be removed -but you want the bond to remain strong- allow them to melt in the sink while you say, "To the earth, to the sea, forever bonded, (your beloved's name) and me."

To come across a pink rose bush blooming in the snow foretells that you will soon be rewarded for your devotion to someone.

Soda pop (carbonated beverage)
If soda pop bubbles out of your nostril after swallowing it is said you have an innocent and childlike nature.

The mixing of brand-name soda pops is considered foolhardy by some, as they say the brand-names will wage war against one another in the digestive track.

If the carbonated bubbles sprinkle into your eyes while drinking a lemon-lime flavored soda pop, any selfless wish you make will be granted.

Men who drink soda pop while eating pickles are thought to have an acerbic sense of humor as well as a high energy level in the lovemaking department.

Spilling a cherry flavored soda pop at a party is thought to attract you admiration from the opposite sex.

For a gerbil to lap at your soda pop is a sign your home is in need of some repair.

To accidentally spill a soda pop on yourself right before a romantic date is warning that your date is in love with someone else.

People who combine carbonated ginger ale with their tea or coffee are said to be thoughtful lovers.

Soap
To drop a soap bar when you're done washing is an omen you will have cause to wash again before the day is through.

Song stuck
Having a song repetitively play in one's mind -or, stuck in one's head- is a common aggravation. To wake up in the morning to be so plagued by a song you haven't heard in a long time means the lyrics or title has special meaning for you on this day.

If the song stuck in your head is one you like but you are tired of it being in your brain, try listening to a song you downright hate.

If the song in your head is strangely one you dislike, it is suggested to listen to *Battle of New Orleans*, which is rumored to have the power of chasing away and keeping away all unwanted stuck tunes.

Star Trek and Star Wars
Almost everyone is familiar with these popular TV and movie series, and there are a few strong beliefs that surround them:

To confuse the name a character from one series with a character from the other is said to mean you are growing senile.

To dream of *Yoda* from Star Wars means you will soon receive some much needed advice.

To dream of Star Trek's *Mr. Spock* is a sign you will soon have a lover who is stoic by personality but fiercely passionate behind closed doors.

If you can make utterances like a Wookiee it is said you will have hairy children.

Praying in Klingon is said to provide you protection from enemies.

Speaking like *Jar Jar Binks* will either fetch you a humiliation in front of a lover, gain you an annoying co-worker or both.

To whisper, "Beam me up, Scotty!" on entering a bar or tavern is said to bring you attention from the prettiest bar maid.

To mispronounce the name of Star Trek character *Data* dooms you to lose a pricey technical device or gadget.

To clap during a scene where *Darth Vader* strangles an admiral will bring you luck at Black Jack. Furthermore, the louder you applaud whenever a storm trooper dies on screen, the more your bowling skills improve.

Sweet-peas
Sweet-pea flowers grown around one's property are thought to invite peace and affection into the home.

Sycamore tree
To stumble or trip beside a Sycamore tree and uttering "Thank you" brings ten years of satisfaction.

Sleeping beneath the boughs of a Sycamore is believed to bring one prophetic visions concerning military conflicts and wars.

Never leave food on the roots of a Sycamore tree unless you want the fairies to take it.

Pouring a libation of wine or milk over Sycamore roots is believed to feed the fairy children.

Tapping or striking someone with a switch made of Sycamore wood is believed to make them unable to lie or hide the truth.

Tattoos
It is believed any woman who gets an anchor tattooed on her stomach will suffer from digestive problems. Contrarily, a man getting an anchor tattoo on his stomach area is said to strengthen his liver. Airline and jet pilots, however, are warned not to get an anchor tattoo anywhere on their body (and for obvious reasons!)

A black panther tattoo on your left shoulder keeps in-laws out of your business.

A sugar skull tattoo on your right buttock is said to draw the protection of dead relatives.

To get an eyeball tattoo on your throat is said to usher in depression and entice hauntings by malicious spirits.

To get a tattoo of your beloved's name will bring a disastrous end of the relationship. To get a tattoo of your beloved's face will bring not only the end of the relationship, but also bring financial disputes between the two of you.

The names of your children tattooed on your arms, back, chest or wrist is said to keep you always fond in their hearts. If your child is dead and you get their name tattooed on your person, their spirits are said to remain close and offer guidance for the rest of your life.

For an old tattoo to bleed indicates someone close to you will undergo a near-fatal experience.

To get a tattoo of the number 27 invites fame tarnished by tragedy.

It is said that if your tattoo artist gets into an argument with someone while doing your tattoo, it won't heal properly.

A tattoo of a female angel smoking a cigarette is supposed to bring extreme good fortune for anyone getting it on their right shoulder blade or the back of either thigh.

For a man to get a tribal tattoo over their left ear will never want for sex.

A woman who has a hummingbird tattoo on a breast will always be fickle in matters of love. However, it is said the woman with a dragon tattoo near a nipple will always be loyal to those she loves.

Blue rose tattoos should never appear on one's ankle as it is said to invite depression.

To get a tattoo of *Keith Richards* (of the Rolling Stones) on the solar plexus is believed to make one invulnerable to the ravages of hard-living.

Getting a tramp stamp tattoo of ivy is said to create an unstable home life. However this can be prevented if images of holly berries are included accompany the ivy.
(See also Wife-Beater Tees)

Teachers
If you have a teacher that makes trouble for you, try the old custom of jumping on his or her shadow. This is said to compel them to change jobs.

To elicit the goodwill of a teacher, take an apple and with your fingernail scratch your initials in the skin. On presenting the apple to the teacher it is believed they will begin seeing you in a favorable light.

A teacher wishing to refrain from cursing around their students is advised to swallow a rose hip.

Tee shirts

Tee shirts have become a staple of the modern wardrobe, and have developed a set of beliefs about the wearing and owning of them:

To inadvertently put your tee shirt on inside-out is said to bring little incidents of bad luck until the shirt is turned right side-out.

Wearing your tee shirt backwards is believed to bring company to the door.

It isn't advised to cut a tag from a tee shirt while wearing it, not just because of safety concerns, but as this is thought to bring on sudden nasty weather in the wearer's proximity.

To wear sandals, eat vegan and drink of a latté while wearing a tee shirt is said to turn you into a hipster.

One should never wear a tee shirt that once belonged to a meth addict, as it is thought to attract demons that will take possession of the new wearer.

Men who wear pink tee shirts while riding a Harley motorcycle are cautioned they will soon lose their women, their companions or both.

Never borrow a friend's tee shirt without washing it by hand before returning. To machine wash or dry clean is thought to rub away the friendship.

Women wearing their man's tee shirt are advised against washing it before he wears it next time. Doing so will cast his eyes toward another, or so it's claimed.

Television (analog set)

If you turn on an old analog TV set (pre-digital generation) and see images of people it is thought these are malevolent and otherworldly entities. You are likewise advised to turn the set off at once.

If you hear your name spoken through an analog signal it is said you will know a year of success followed by two years of embarrassing events.

The Twilight Zone (television series)
Take care in quoting from *The Twilight Zone*, as it is said the attempt to flirt with anyone by using such a quote makes your truest nature obvious to the other person.

The Wizard of Oz (books and film)
Good luck is said to follow all day if you say "Dorothy Gale" before rising from bed in the morning.

Giving a newborn a book from the Oz series by Frank L. Baum is said to grant the child a humorous wit, a prosperous future and the ability to know when someone is lying to them.

To draw favor from your gods: Mute the volume on your television set. Start playing *The Wizard of Oz* movie at the exact time you begin playing Pink Floyd's *Dark Side of The Moon* album.

To make a spiteful neighbor leave you alone, it is advised to send them a copy (CD or otherwise) of the classic *The Wizard of Oz* film. This act must be done anonymously in order to be effective.

Keeping in your home a photograph of Judy Garland (Dorothy) holding Toto is said to keep you and your loved ones safe from twisters.

Financial gain is said to be had if you keep a tiny pair of silver(colored) shoes hidden in your chimney (unlike on film, in the books the shoes of the bad witch's shoes were silver).

To use a tablecloth made of same blue gingham pattern Judy Garland wore in *The Wizard of Oz* is said to keep peace during family meals. Likewise, to keep a filled oil can (like that of the Tin Man's) near your front door is said to attract love to your door. And keeping straw outside your door is thought to keep *humbug* salesmen away.

Thunderbird
If you are one of the rare people blessed to glimpse the legendary Thunderbird (in flight or otherwise), be assured good fortune is coming to you and your family. To track the Thunderbird, however, is never advised as calamity befalls anyone arrogant enough to spy on a Thunderbird, their offspring or nest.

Tic-Tac-Toe (game of Noughts and Crosses)
If you are playing the O's (Noughts) and your opponent dies before the game is officially ended, it is said you will be their next acquaintance to enter the after-life. But if you are playing the X's (Crosses) and your opponent meets such a death, it is believed you will be the last of their acquaintances to die.

Tin
To eat off tin plates is believed to attract earth elements. And if you own tin plates and care for them, it is said these earth elements will stand guard over your property.

Tipping
You will experience a poor night's sleep if you tip a bell hop with filthy bills.

You will soon find yourself falsely accused if the tip you leave a waitress is all in pennies.

Your manicure and/or pedicure will last longer if you hand the salon worker their tip in a light yellow colored envelope.

It is said you should always give parking valets their tips in rounded figures to prevent a tire blow out on the way home.

Giving the busboy a cigarette along with a tip will prevent your meal from causing indigestion.

To leave the server's tip on a saucer at your table invites good will among the restaurant employees.

To bicker with a companion over who leaves the tip will cause the aromas from the restaurant's kitchen to turn bad.

It is thought that to tip your garbage man (or woman) will drive vermin from your home.

If you tip a grocery store employee you will soon be invited out to dinner.

Toads
Coming across a dead and flattened toad on the highway or road is a warning you are headed toward danger.

A toad appearing on your windowsill is a sign that your woes will soon be replaced by laughter and good times.

To see a toad catch a spider is a sign your endurance will soon be tested by a villainous person. If the toad eats the spider, be assured you will triumph over a coming evil.

Toilet tissue
If when at home you use up the last of a toilet tissue roll and leave it to the next person in the bathroom to replace it, you will suffer a stomach ache before bedtime.

If you encounter a rabbi with tissue paper stuck on his shoe, it is suggested you wish him a good day lest he suffer a fall with injury on the way home.

It is said you can get someone fired from their job by writing their name three times on a sheet of toilet tissue and then flush this down the toilet.

If a pet knocks over a wastebasket containing used toilet tissue (or facial tissue), expect company before the end of the day.

If you use toilet tissue to clean mud or debris from any of your car windows, expect it to return three-fold.

Tomatoes
The tomato is a good source of vitamin C and anti-oxidants. In addition to these benefits, some people stuff their pillows with dried tomato seeds, thinking this keeps cold viruses at bay.

The year's first tomato from your garden should be offered freely to a woman, as the tomato is thought to be sacred to Venus.

Tortoise shell
The tortoise is revered as a sacred animal in many cultures, and the shell of a tortoise that died naturally is considered to hold the vibrations of the divine.

To groom an infant's fine hair with a tortoise shell comb is said to confer on the child the blessings from the divine.

To share with another a meal served on a tortoise shell dish is said to make the bonds between you everlasting.

To burn sage in a tortoise shell bowl is deemed to be a most holy act that cleanses the physical plane and also shows reverence to one's ancestors.

Toupees
To come across an abandoned toupee ushers in a host of misfortunes. To pass the same toupee along to someone else is said to likewise pass the misfortune along. To rid yourself altogether of the bad vibes from the abandoned toupee, it is recommended to burn it.

Travel lodging (inns, motels, hotels, ect.)
While it is common among travelers and vacationers to take towels, ashtrays, cups or other items from a place of lodging by simple fault of packing overlook. Others, however, practice the

taking of such items as souvenirs, and some believe such a souvenir -when taken during an enjoyable stay- carries the good times with it.

In parts of North America, it is regarded as sacrilegious to Native beliefs to take lodging in a place that outright prohibits the smoking or other uses of tobacco.

Common is the notion that rooms where a murder or suicide happened are haunted.

One postulation suggests that if you purposely bring to a lodging the trash accumulated from elsewhere and leave it for the maid to take out, your property will be unsightly by other people's messes when you return home..

Tree stump
Finding a robin's nest with eggs in a tree stump is a harbinger of better days if the eggs are left unmolested.

To find the hair or tail of a squirrel on a tree stump is a warning the coming winter will be harsh.

The discovery of milk or holly berries on a tree stump is a sign the fairies favor you.

Coming across a willow sapling growing from the stump of an oak means the gods will provide you companionship in old age.

Tune stuck (see Song stuck)

Turkey (Wild Turkeys, Meleagris)
The meat of these large fowl are considered by many to possess healing qualities. Occasionally eating a meal of turkey (thoroughly cooked) is believed by some to help alleviate pain in the intestinal track and to promote bowel movements. Due to the levels of tryptophan found in turkey meat, eating a large meal of it is asserted to produce drowsiness and a good night's rest. On the other hand, however, over-consumption of turkey meat is believed to induce constipation. (*Caution: seek the*

advice of your medical practitioner before consuming turkey meat for any medical condition!)

Feathers of the wild turkey are regarded as strong amulets in the area of psychic defenses. Sleeping on a pillow stuffed with wild turkey feathers is thought to promote defense against nightmares and dreams forced to you by the will of another person. Some Native Americans use turkey feathers in the practice of cleansing smudges, especially in cases where unknown negative forces physically plague the victim.

Turul bird
Dreams of the Turul bird of Magyar legend are said to be prophetic visions about the dreamer's descendants. As these visions are believed to come directly from the Creator, he or she who dreams of this great bird are encouraged to pay attention to the details of the vision in order to interpret the message. *(see also Thunderbird)*

Ultrasound (in vitro ultrasound)
If your child is serving in the military, kissing their ultrasound picture and then keeping it in a purple frame or one set with purple crystals is supposed to make them clear-headed in battle and to help them elude capture by the enemy.

Umbrella
Many football fans believe that when their team plays at a rival team's home turf, bringing an umbrella along to the game increases the chance of weather unfavorable to the rival team.

Unicorn
Sightings of the legendary unicorn are rarely reported today, but here are a few things worth bearing in mind if you are fortunate enough to see this creature:

For a unicorn to approach you outdoors means you have been noticed for being someone who respects both nature and the old (pagan) ways.

If a woman past her child-bearing days is visited by a unicorn, it is said she will give birth to a child who will claim lasting renown.

A child that sees a unicorn can be expected to grow up with profound wisdom and tolerance.

Uni-brow
Today when a person's eyebrows meet over the bridge of the nose they are often said to have a uni-brow. Over the centuries numerous (and often unkind) superstitions arose about people born with uni-brows, and some of these survive today. Among these superstitions:

Having a uni-brow is a sign you are a werewolf.

Men with uni-brows are over-sexed.

Women with uni-brows are more *mannish* than most.

Babies born with uni-brows can expect a life tempted by the devil at every turn.

A uni-brow is indicative of a brutish nature and low intellectual capacities.

People with uni-brows are charismatic by personality and criminal by agenda.

By contradiction there are a few positive superstitions about uni-brows, too, and these include:
People with uni-brows possess a high level of natural empathy for their fellow man.

Riches and fortune are easily obtained by those born with a uni-brow.

Uni-brow people are more energetic lovers.

Those born with uni-brows are more in tune with the Earth than others.

Valentine's Day candy
To put your sweetheart in the mood for some lov'in, be sure to present their Valentine's Day candy in black tissue wrap.

Valentine's Day cookies
To attract the love of someone, share with them a heart-shaped (Valentine) cookie that you've made yourself. And to keep your sweetheart faithful, add ground orange rind to the icing.

Giving someone a broken Valentine's Day cookie is said to attract rivals for your sweetheart's affections.

Giving Valentine's Day cookies to children is believed to make them merciful.

Vanity Plates
To acquire a vanity plate that boasts about your business or brand is said to make you unpopular with clients and customers. Any physician who gets such a vanity plate is warned criminal charges will enter their future.

Vanity plates once owned by celebrities can be highly sought at auctions. But you may wish to bear in mind the following before purchase: vanity plates once owned by anyone who died in a vehicular accident are reputed to carry the dark vibrations of the accident with them.

Pet enthusiasts recommend not getting your pet's name put on a vanity plate as this may put your animal at risk for being hit by a vehicle.

Vapes
It is warned that to criticize anyone for using a vape (electronic cigarette) invites lung cancer to visit itself upon you.

Velcro (closures)
As much as a modern convenience velcro closures may be, using them does come with certain cultural warnings:

People over the age of 20 and who wear shoes with velcro straps are said to age prematurely.

Womens garments with velcro closures are said to last only half as long as the same garment than come with a different type of closures.

You may expect inconveniences from co-workers if you discover the velcro on your apparel is mussed with lint.

Velvet
Ladies, when looking for love, consider wearing a choker made of blue velvet as blue velvet is thought to have the power of bringing the notice of true gentlemen to the wearer. A blue velvet cuff worn on the left wrist is also said to have this effect.

Some singers wear skirts or trousers made of purple velvet while performing as it is believed to help the audience appreciative of their style and talent.

Black velvet sewn into the waistband and leg openings of undergarments is said to arouse and increase desire from one's lover.

Placing one's valuable in a carrying pouch of brown velvet is thought to dispossess the article of negative vibrations. Leave the item in the velvet for at least 48 hours, then burn or bury the pouch after use.

Some people wrap or skirt their holiday evergreens in a bolt of green velvet, believing this will keep the needles supple longer.

Virgins
There have been many ever-changing superstitions regarding virgins throughout the last hundred years or so. Among the charms and superstitions put forth today (and a few are rather humorous):

Virgins under the age of 17 are warned not to have orange colored rubber wrist bands used to show support for a cause, as these are more likely to bring about misunderstandings with friends. If you are a virgin of this age group, it is recommended to wear yellow or green such rubber wrist bands.

A virgin can cure bladder infections and kidney ailments by touching the afflicted while they -the afflicted- is sitting in a bubble bath.

A virgin that climbs a ladder to get onto a roof will soon be sexually active unless they fall off before reaching the roof.

Spotting a virgin
For a young woman to routinely sit with her legs together or crossed indicates she is a virgin (to sit with one's legs parted supposedly means they are no longer virgins - and more, if the young woman tends to lean forward with their legs parted is said to mean they are pregnant).

It requires a state of virginity to be able to recite aloud, in precise chronological order, the entire *Star Wars* storyline.

The wearing of pearl earrings to a school dance is said to be more common among virgins than non-virgins.

Non-virgins are believed to double-dip their chips.

Virgins never buy tampons.

Virgins have a custom of repetitiously dunking their tea bags.

When making peanut butter and banana sandwiches, a virgin cuts the bananas in circular slices; the non-virgin slices their bananas length-wise.

The more icons a female under the age of 18 has on her computer monitor, the more likely she is to be a virgin. By contrast, in women over 30, the more icons she has, the more kinky techniques she is said to practice.

Virgins lick their ice cream cones upward, while non-virgins use a swirling tongue technique.

Vitamin A (supplements)
A diet containing the proper daily allowance of vitamin A is essential for good health. This may explain why some people believe that dropping a vitamin A capsule means you should get your eyes examined. Others maintain, however, that for your vitamin A supplement to leak in your palm is a sign someone you fancy will soon take notice!

Voting
To trip on the way out of a voting booth signifies you will have second thoughts about the candidate who just got your vote.

It is a sign you used good judgment if your strong hand tingles after exiting the voting booth.

To pass a dead chicken, a hearse and a homeless person either on the way to or from the voting booth is an omen of dire national tribulations following the election.

Weddings
It is said that to wear the color fuchsia at your own wedding will make your partner fickle.

For a groom to drink from the same cup or glass as his mother-in-law denotes they will get along in the future.

To cram a piece of wedding cake in your spouse's face invites matrimonial disaster.

For a groom to buy or rent his suit from the same shop as his father-in-law denotes future rivalry between them.

Anyone who texts during a wedding ceremony is put at risk to be soaked by rain and pelted by hail.

Brides should never wear plastic or rubber shoes or sandals to their wedding as this is said to invite betrayals in the marriage.

Orange blossoms arranged at the wedding banquet table are thought to usher in happiness for the newlyweds.

When it comes to the wedding music selections, it is widely felt that Bobby Brown tunes should never be played. However, the inclusion of "Love Is Like A Butterfly" by Dolly Parton welcomes in a tender honeymoon.

For the groom to kiss the first child he sees after exchanging vows is said to boost the bride's fertility.

Wedding ring
If your wedding ring falls off while bathing or showering, expect your spouse to face peril in the near future.

If your wedding ring gets caught in your hair, it is said someone is jealous of your matrimonial bliss.

On finding an old wedding ring in a new residence, know that kindly spirits are glad you are there.

Widow's peak (hair line)
For many centuries, people born with a widow's peak were said destined to outlive their spouses. Today, those with widow's peaks are also attributed with a natural affinity for practicing the magical arts.

However there are a few other modern beliefs:
Dark-skinned people with kinky hair and a widow's peak are believed to be destined for glory.

Fair-skinned people with naturally dark hair and a widow's peak are rumored to associate with vampires.

Red-haired people with widow peaks are thought to have unusually high sex drives.

Natural blondes with widow peaks are cautioned to keep their guard against scoundrels who would take advantage of their generous nature.

People born with widow's peaks are able to cast out and control demons.

Men who have lost their widow peak due to baldness will be both envied and esteemed by their male heirs.

Wife-beater tees (tee-shirts)
To wear a wife-beater to a wedding denotes you will soon be arrested.

To get tattooed while wearing a wife-beater brings about disappointment in love. Additionally, to get a tribal tattoo on your arm while wearing a wife-beater augurs an arrest in the near future.

To accidentally spill a purple-colored drink on your wife-beater will bring you unexpected fame.

To be unintentionally filmed wearing a wife-beater while entering a dentist's office is said to bring notoriety.

Any woman wanting to borrow her husband's wife-beater should always kiss the inside of it before putting it on, otherwise there will soon be arguments with a neighbor.

White Mustang (car)
Legend has it that unmarried people should avoid driving white Ford Mustangs as to do so will soon involve them in legal hassles. By contrast, married people purchasing such a vehicle can look forward to improved finances.

Willow
For a willow sapling to appear growing in your lettuce bed means you can expect the arrival of pleasant new neighbors.

To see a willow press against a strong wind indicates you will be granted endurance in an upcoming challenge.

A willow trunk cleaved by a lightning strike and which continues to grow is thought a nature spirit in disguise.

Wolf
The reputation of wolves was tarnished for a very long time by prejudicial stereotypes and frightful fairy tales. Today the trend has thankfully reversed, and most people regard wolves as the noble, family-devoted creatures they are. With this trend have evolved new beliefs surrounding this beautiful animal:

To sight a lone wolf outdoors is thought a sign of coming good fortune.

If you are lucky enough to meet a wolf's eyes, you will at once feel the presence of that great Creator of us all.

For a wolf to lick your hand is a sign you have been forgiven for some dark transgression.

For a pack of wolves to run across your path is a message you need to throw off the bonds of convention.

Hearing the howling of a single wolf is sign you have an important choice that needs to be made. The howling of several wolves augurs that you will have the support of loyal friends in troubling times ahead.

Woolly Worms (Isabella tiger moth larvae)
This fuzzy caterpillar with its coloring of black ends with a rusty or brown central band is well-recognized in many parts of the world. North American weather watchers are also acquainted with the caterpillar, when seen in the autumn time, as a predictor of weather. When the caterpillar's central band is long, or wide, the coming winter will be mild. When the central band is short or if the caterpillar is completely black, winter is sure to be a severe one.

Wonky digital display and reception
Do you remember some years back when the government decided that digital movie videos were so gosh darned awesome that they forced analog programming to be replaced by digital? We viewers were promised these digital transmissions would be bolder, clearer and better, and the fact is yes, yesteryear's viewing irritations of bleeding shadows and snow have gone the way of the dinosaurs. Alas, they have been replaced by the all-too-familiar problem already prevalent in the videos - that of wonky digital displays. If you hate display and reception wonk, some ideas have emerged on how these problems can be resolved:

Walking in front of your television is often blamed for producing the wonky imagery, so if you have to make a visit to any other room in the house, pause the programming first.

Some contend that demons are responsible for the wonk, so having your television exorcized by a priest, minister, rabbi or other religiously ordained person will get rid your set of the problem.

Playing rap music is said by some to annoy sensitive televisions, so avoid playing it in your home. Still others contend that one should never listen to classical music, country & western, rock, show tunes or even gospel around a television set or wonk will inevitably occur. (In other words, just don't listen to music in the privacy of the home or your precious television will suffer!)

Slamming drawers and cabinet doors are thought to clear up digital wonk.

Living near a power transformer has been blamed for the problem as well, so if there is a transformer near your home, you can always move.

Heat has also been blamed for digital wonk, so be sure to live somewhere cold.

The following activities are also suspected of interfering with digital reception, so you may consider avoiding them altogether: eating, talking, yawning, coughing, passing gas, laughing, smiling, scratching, yoga, kissing, making love, answering a phone call, doing school work, flushing a toilet, feeding a fish, scratching, blinking. (*Note: in this author's opinion, if it requires avoidance of any of these activities to get a better reception, a much wiser approach to the problem is to turn off the television and just read a book.*)

Wood (knocking on)

Knocking on wood for good luck is an old custom, but the modern superstition surrounding this practice has evolved into a distinct little procedure - namely, when speaking of an unthinkable scenario, one is advised to immediately afterward knock on wood so that exact scenario does not come about.

Yawning

If you yawn three times in a row without shedding a single tear, you are encouraged to snap your fingers three times or very soon you'll have a real reason to shed tears.

YouTube
(see Internet)

Zebra

This member of the Equidae family is recognized the world over for its distinctive striped patterned coat and typically gentle nature. Most zebras remain free and untamed, and perhaps it is for this reason that some claim that wearing zebra-print fabric or carrying an image of a zebra lends one the essence of the *un-tamable.*

Making love on Zebra-print bed sheets are thought to imbue lovers with a sense of wild abandon.

II.   Miscellaneous Charmwork

Attracting love

When wanting to attract love into your life without enslaving somebody's feelings, you want to make yourself worthy in the eyes of the Love spirits/deities. A simple way to achieve this: find or gather six pink stones or crystals, and wash them under clear running water. Now fill your tub with warm water and get into the tub along with your six pink stones. Luxuriate for at least thirty minutes while imagining yourself embraced by the arms of true love. Remove the stones and get out and dry. Without cleaning or polishing the stones again, place them in the windows of your residence, being sure to leave the windows open. This procedure should draw Love to you soon, if you are meant to have it.

Cleansing your home of unwanted spirits

Burning sage and fanning the smoke is ancient method of banishing unwanted spirits and demonic forces, and this practice is still popular today. Be sure to burn the sage in a non-porous, non-flammable container, and fan the sage smoke with a feather (preferably one from an eagle, hawk or other high-soaring bird). In this way distribute the smoke throughout your residence or working area. Pay special attention to doorways, windows and open chimneys. One may also *smudge* or spiritually cleanse themselves or others by wafting the smoke over the body.
Caution: never leave sage burning unattended, and do not get burning sage near hair or flammable material. Be sure to open windows for fresh air following the procedure.

Communicating with the dead

One may communicate safely with departed souls by obtaining the skull of a horse that was slain on the battlefield. Set the skull in a place of honor, then cleanse the area by burning sandalwood or sage incense. Place near the skull -but not in the incense- offerings of alfalfa blossoms to show honor to the spirit of the horse.. Meditate on the horse's spirit and ask it to lead you to the departed one you wish to contact. If you are able to converse with the spirit you sought, be sure to thank the horse's spirit afterward. Complete this ritual by offering the spirit kernels of dried corn or an apple, then thank it for its aid and wish it a good journey back to the realm of the dead.

Consolation of grief
The softening of grief is thought possible by tossing autumn leaves into a running stream while thinking of the departed one being happy in their afterlife.

Pagans of northern European descent often invoke the name of the goddess *Nanna* for consolation in times of grief. (Nanna is the wife of the Norse Christ-like god, Baldur)

Dispelling Bad Luck
Wearing an elephant charm on the right wrist is believed to dispel bad luck.

On seeing a June bug or dragonfly, quietly make a wish for good luck to enter your life. It is believed the insect will carry your plea straight to the realms of your gods. This action will prove futile, however, if you have accumulated a lot of bad karma.

Driving away a stalker
If you suspect you are being stalked but have no proof, try wearing a brown length of cord from which is hung a broken piece of seashell. To enhance the power of this amulet, smear your solar plexus with the juice of fresh mugwort leaves. This is thought to turn a stalker's thoughts away from you. *(In the event you discover proof of a stalker, contact the authorities at once and ask for advice on what legal safety measures should be taken!)*

Getting a good night's sleep
Drinking a cup of chamomile tea is a popular method of relaxing and getting shut eye.

Some suggest stuffing your pillow with catnip leaves or violet petals to encourage a good night's sleep. Others rely on burning yellow rose petals as incense in the room before lying down.

Once the petals have burned and all flames extinguished, it is believed you may lie down for blissful rest.

Good luck in court
Some people believe a favorable verdict in court can be had by carrying a lock of hair from a meth addict who has been arrested at least three times. The lock of hair must be freely given by the addict for the charm to work.

In Nevada, some contend that kissing a photograph of *Wayne Newton* prior to going to court will bring favor from the judge or jury.

To avoid the displeasure of a judge, never carry a cell phone into court.

Some contend that to be fairly treated in a child custody case, you should make an anonymous donation to an animal shelter prior to the proceedings. Likewise, petting a puppy and offering it tidbits of bacon before appearing in court is said to win you the favor of lady justice in matters of child custody.

If you are a singer or belong to a band and find yourself faced with a lawsuit related to the music industry, it is suggested to listen to Led Zeppelin's *Stairway To Heaven*   just before entering the court room.

To win a dismissal in a charge of music copyright infringement, it is recommended to snap your fingers seven times in succession while repeating the maiden name of your maternal grandmother (your mother's mother).

To win a case when you are innocent of the charge, it is suggested you wear clothing of warm -but not overly dark- blue shades throughout the trial. However, the wearing of aqua or turquoise shades during a trial is said to bring about a hung jury verdict and the risk of re-trial.

If you are guilty of the charge and still hope for a favorable verdict, it is suggested that during the trial you wear undergarments with the name *Michael Corleone* stitched with gold thread on them.

Help in recuperation after illness
To help in recovery from a simple illness, suck on a lemon slice first thing in the morning.

Drinking a cup of warm chai tea before bedtime is said to help to recover from colds and flu.

To dispel the remnants of any illness lingering about, it is a habit of some to slice an onion in half and keep these pieces in the central area of the dwelling. Leave out for three days; do not eat nor allow children or animals to partake of the onion. When the three days have passed, bury the onion parts in the earth on the western portion of your property.

Hope
To gain hope when all seems lost, find a piece of yellow or golden quartz. Wash the quartz under clear running water, dry with a clean cloth and carry with you at all times. When feelings of doubt come over you, touch the quartz with your left hand; massage if needed.

Some Christians, to find hope in trying times, open the Bible to a random page, and with their eyes closed, place a forefinger to a page. Upon opening their eyes they read aloud the verse their finger has touched, then say Amen.

Improving vision
Some people maintain that reading passages from the Bible without aid of glasses or contacts will improve the eyesight. Others suggest typing the name *Stephen King* 99 times by use of an electric typewriter in order to obtain clearer vision.

Liberation from a miserable situation
It is suggested by some *Harry Potter* fans that liberation from a bad, miserable or overwhelming problem may be achieved by invoking the name of the character Dobby in the following way: upon going to bed, mentally repeat the name Dobby over and

over until you fall asleep. Perform this mental invocation three nights in a row to to secure your liberation.

Privacy
Wearing something with a mint-green plaid design is believed to keep nosy people out of your personal affairs.

To keep your illicit practices proverbially under the radar, carrying a tiny piece of iron screen is recommended. This charm is said to work best if the screen has been breathed on by a person who smokes tobacco.

Making snoops unwilling to enter your residence is believed achievable by burying a small piece of iron at the furthermost four quadrants of the property. After burying the pieces of iron, spit three times on the earth covering each individual piece.

Protection against intruders
Placing the bones of a beloved pet near your front door helps in protecting the home from intruders. Be sure to offer flowers at the grave often.

A bolt or strip of plaid cloth hung on the outside of all doors is thought to make intruders think twice before entering.

Burying a dead skunk near your front drive is also thought helpful in keeping the unwanted from approaching your home.

Protection from radical religious ideology/ideologists
If you are fearful of danger from radical religious ideologists, this protective charm bag may help bring give peace of mind. Get the following items:

Small white (never previously used) medicine bag-type pouch
A miniature glass bottle or vessel of wine with a well-fitted and adequate stopper
A piece of dried pork
Three hairs of a dog
Length of white cord

Place the glass container of wine, the dried pork and the dog hairs into the pouch, kiss the pouch while thinking of the Virgin Mary or other female Patron (deity) you feel close to. Attach this amulet to the white cord and wear it around the neck, making sure the pouch hangs just over your solar plexus. Meditate and pray often to your female Patron; asking for Her protection against violence and persecution from fanatics.

Rain
Popular theory holds that when rain is sought, park your car outdoors and wash it so the rain is sure to arrive.

Reconciliation with a friend
Offering your friend a grilled cheese sandwich is thought to reconcile an on-the-skids relationship.

Unraveling a mystery
To unravel a mystery that has plagued you, it is said that by binge watching the television series *Monk* the truth will be revealed!

About the author:
As an author and guest contributor Beth Perry has written extensively on the subjects of folklore, legends and the paranormal for books, blogs and television. She also pens adult fiction under the pseudonym Anya Howard, and is an active member of the U.S. Norse and Aesirvolk community. Beth Perry makes her home with her family in the scenic foothills of Tennessee. Readers are invited to visit her on the web at http://bethperry.weebly.com or the website of her pseudonym at anyahoward.com

.

www.ingramcontent.com/pod-product-compliance
Lightning Source LLC
Chambersburg PA
CBHW070155290526
45789CB00002B/785